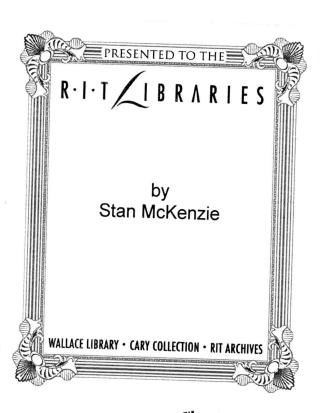

Color Separation on the Desktop

How to Get Good Color Reproductions

Miles Southworth
and
Donna Southworth

Tom Plough
With my thanks for your support.
Miles Southworth
11/93

Graphic Arts Publishing
Livonia, NY 14487-9716

Printed in the United States of America
ISBN 0-933600-08-9
Library of Congress Card No. 93-073114

First printing October 1993

Credits

Printed by Cohber Press, Rochester, NY
Bound by Riverside Group, Rochester, NY
Cover design by Gregory North
Production assistance by Andrew Chen, Andrea Clough, Gregory North and Jim Rich

Dedicated to our parents

Kathryn and Donald Burley
Deane and Dwight Southworth

Table of Contents

About the authors

Miles Southworth is a leading color printing technology authority. He is the Roger K. Fawcett Distinguished Professor of Publication Color Management at the Rochester Institute of Technology (RIT), School of Printing Management and Sciences (SPMS). Southworth is the author of several articles and books (see the list of additional books on page viii). He is past president of the Technical Association of the Graphic Arts (TAGA) and is a member of the International Association of Graphic Arts Consultants. Since 1981, Miles and Donna Southworth have published *The Quality Control Scanner*, a monthly newsletter on color reproduction and quality.

Donna Southworth is vice president, secretary and treasurer of Graphic Arts Publishing Inc. She manages most functional areas of the publishing business. Working closely with Miles Southworth, she is actively involved in writing, editing and publishing literature for the graphic arts industry.

Foreword

Around the world, the desktop computer has become the tool for page makeup. Typesetting and page assembly used to be done manually and, more recently, with color electronic prepress systems (CEPS). Now, typesetting and page assembly are done on a desktop computer, the Macintosh or PC (personal computer), and output to film on imagesetters. In the past, halftones and color separations were made on highend scanners and manually stripped into the pages. Now, images are scanned electronically and, before the films are made, placed in the pages using the desktop computer and appropriate software.

Over the last 50 years, the graphic arts industry has learned to produce good color. Graphic arts professionals know what it takes for any printing conditions. Now, the desktop computer operator must learn how to get good color separations and resulting good color reproductions. This book presents professional secrets that you, the desktop computer operator or scanner operator, need to know. Enough information is included to enable you to be successful in producing professional looking color reproductions. By following the procedures presented, you can produce good color every time.

After years of research and experience, people working in the graphic arts industry know how to control print quality on the press, regardless of how a job is printed. If calibrated devices and correct procedures are followed, there are no surprises at the press—"What you get is what you saw on the monitor and on the color proof." The results of the printing are only as good as the films that were supplied for the printing process. The responsibility for good films belongs to the person making up the page. If you are that person, you must insure that the correct color separations are produced.

There is a growing demand for color reproduction. In today's market, it is very cost-effective to produce color in pages that once were printed only in black and white. This puts even more responsibility on designers and graphic arts professionals to understand how to reproduce good color. If you prepare electronic copy for reproduction by a printing process, then you need this skill.

ADDITIONAL PUBLICATIONS
BY THESE AUTHORS

Color Separation Techniques, 3rd edition
Miles Southworth

Pocket Guide to Color Reproduction, 3rd edition
Miles Southworth

Quality and Productivity in the Graphic Arts
Miles Southworth
Donna Southworth
with chapters by Eisner, Killmon,
Layne, Marathe and Rebsamen

How to Implement Total Quality Management
Miles Southworth
Donna Southworth

The Quality Control Scanner,
since 1981, a monthly newsletter about
color reproduction and quality control
Miles Southworth, Co-editor
Donna Southworth, Co-editor

The Color Resource Complete Color Glossary
Miles Southworth
Thad McIlroy
Donna Southworth

WHAT IS GOOD COLOR?

What's necessary for good desktop color

The difference between a good color reproduction and a poor color reproduction is usually the result of:

- the color scanner chosen by the operator,
- the proper scanner or desktop computer setup for the printing parameters,
- the original's image and emulsion characteristics, and
- the scanner operator's image adjustment for a good visual reproduction.

Learn what is needed and you can always make good color reproductions. Keep in mind the following phrase:

Clean and bright is always right
Dull and gray is not the way

Let this phrase be your guiding principle for good, clean color reproductions.

What customers expect color reproductions to look like

People count on good printed color reproductions to have correct contrast and color balance. They want the colors to be bright, clean and saturated. The picture should appear clear, sharp, and focused with the detail showing. People also expect memory colors to be accurate. *Memory colors* are blue sky, green grass, red apples, and items, such as fruits and vegetables, that people easily remember.

What customers don't want to see

No one wants to think that they are looking at a picture through a dirty screen door or window glass. The picture should not appear flat without contrast. Deep, saturated colors should not appear pale or washed out. People in the picture should not appear ashen or sunburned. Caucasians should be tan and slightly warm; African Americans should be a warm, even brown. Nothing in the picture should have a color cast that makes it appear too blue, green or red.

Fuzzy, out of focus or out of register reproduced images are undesirable. Large blobs of color with no detail and excess graininess in reproductions also cause customers to complain.

REPRODUCING COLOR

All color starts with light

Color is a visual sensation that involves a light source, colored objects and a human observer's eyes and brain. These elements interact with one another to produce the color sensation. The human eye is sensitive to red light, green light and blue light. The object absorbs a portion of the light illuminating it and reflects a portion to the observer's eyes. The color seen is dependent on how much red, green and blue light reaches the eyes. Objects in low light levels can be seen. However, the eyes are unable to detect color. Years ago a famous artist said, "All color looks the same in the dark." He was very observant indeed.

Any object appears colored because it possesses pigments or dyes that either absorb, transmit or reflect some portion of the light illuminating it. The object's color depends on the illuminating light's color. The visual effect can be quite different depending on the condition of the object, light source, viewing conditions and observer.

The light quality reaching the observer's eyes determines what color the object appears. Therefore, anything that changes the illuminating light's color, also changes the color of the reflected light and thus changes the perceived color seen by the observer. This explains why standard viewing conditions with a constant light color and intensity are important for consistency when evaluating color at different locations, evaluating press sheets at different time intervals, comparing the original with the proof, or comparing the press sheet with the OK proof.[1]

Color attributes

Color has three important attributes, *hue*, *saturation* and *brightness*. All three are controlled to produce color reproductions.

Hue describes the "color" of a color, whether it is red, green, blue, cyan, magenta, yellow, chartreuse, aqua or another descriptor. Hue results from the dominant light wavelength.

Saturation describes the color's strength and its departure from gray. The color's saturation may vary from strong to weak. An example of changing saturation is adding pigment to a clear ink vehicle. As more pigment is added the color increases in saturation. The hue does not change, but the strength increases.

Brightness describes a color's lightness or darkness, regardless of the color's saturation or hue. For example, a very saturated red can be either very dark like a rich wine or bright like a red geranium.

Additive color theory describes how light colors added together produce other colors. If the rainbow is divided into approximate thirds, the three predominant colors are red, green and blue light.

---

[1] *OK proof*, also called a *color OK*, is a proof of the set of separations that has been evaluated and accepted by the customer. The customer then expects the printed reproduction to look like this proof. The OK proof is used for color quality control for the rest of the pressrun.

To demonstrate the additivity of these three colors, project a red light, a green light and a blue light onto a white surface. Where all three colors overlap, the observer has the sensation of white. Where only two of the light colors overlap, the resulting color is cyan, magenta or yellow. When no light illuminates the white surface, the result is black. Differing amounts of all three additive colors produce what is called the *visible spectrum*, or *color gamut*. The visible spectrum, or color gamut, indicates the full color range that the human eye can perceive.

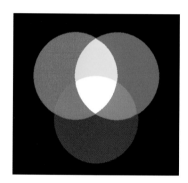 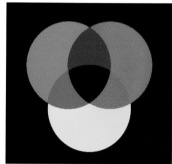

Figure 1 Additive color red, green and blue light

Figure 2 Subtractive color cyan, magenta and yellow pigments

Reproducing colors with pigments and inks on a white surface

The *subtractive color process* is used in printing color reproductions on a white substrate, such as paper. All of the color that is going to be visible on paper is already on it. White paper is white because all the white light shining on its surface reflects back to the human eyes. The red, green and blue light portions added together make white light.

In the four-color printing process, color is created on the substrate by using three transparent pigments, cyan, magenta and yellow inks, as filters. They are called *process colors* or *process inks* and are usually identified using the capital letters C, M and Y. Each absorbs one third of the visible spectrum and transmits two thirds.

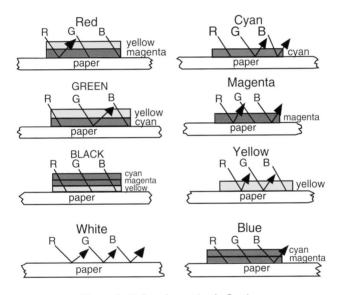

Figure 3 Color absorption/reflection

In other words, the ink pigments subtract some of the light. Cyan ink absorbs red light. Magenta ink absorbs green light. Yellow ink absorbs blue light. When red light is absorbed, green and blue light is reflected, and the observer sees cyan. When green light is absorbed, the red and blue light is reflected and the observer sees magenta. When the blue light is absorbed, the red and green light is reflected and the observer sees yellow. The inks absorb a portion of the light and the paper reflects the unabsorbed portions to the observer's eyes. Note: with process colors, the paper reflects the light, not the inks. This means that the paper surface plays a major role in the color's appearance. See the subtractive color illustration in Figure 2.

If any two of the process inks are printed together, they absorb two thirds of the visible spectrum and create overprint colors of red (R), green (G) or blue (B). If all three inks are printed over one another, all light is absorbed resulting in black. However, in actual practice the three-color overprint appears brown. It is not as dark as desired. Therefore, to achieve the shadow area darkness, a black ink is printed. Since black is referred to as the Key, the black in four-color process is identified with the capital letter "K". This prevents confusion with the "B" for blue.

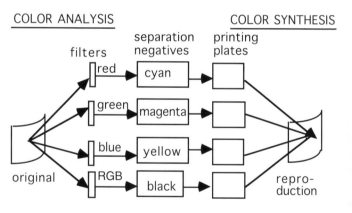

Figure 4 The four-color printing process

Process inks are not pure colors. Therefore, when you are making color halftone separations, you have to make minor corrections for the unwanted contamination. This problem is addressed later in this book, see Color correction, page 49.

Hue, saturation and brightness

Using most printing processes, it is impossible to match the original colors in the reproduction by varying the ink thicknesses. The various hues, saturations and brightnesses are created by printing each process color with varying-sized halftone dots. In digital systems, these dots are electronically generated during film output. From 0 to 100 percent dot sizes for each process color are printed in any area of the reproduction. In any given area, from 0 percent dot to 400 percent dot may be printed. If 100 percent of all four colors print in one area, 400 percent dot happens.

These dots are so small that the human eye cannot resolve them without a magnifying glass. The color that is seen is the result of the combined light absorbed by the ink dots and the light reflected by the paper. The reflected light has been blended into a color with a given hue, saturation and brightness. The fact that this light mixture is seen, and not the dots, is called *mosaic fusion*.

Color balance

A color reproduction should appear to have each color strength correct relative to all other color strengths. Once each color's correct dot sizes, or ink amount, is determined for color balance, the balance must be maintained. If one color becomes too heavy, it may produce a color cast. When color control adjustments are made, color balance is more important to hue consistency than the exact amount of color strength.

Printing color halftone separations

Today, a color scanner is used to make color halftone separations of the original transparency or reflective images. The colors of the original are divided into the four process colors, CMYK. This information is modified for imperfections in the original, a given set of printing conditions and the customer's desires. Halftone separations are made with varying-sized halftone dots on film for printing. It is confusing that halftone separations are also referred to as film separations and halftone screens, or simply as films, halftones, separations, screens and printers.

If the four halftone separations were printed directly over one another, an objectionable pattern, called *moiré*, would result. To minimize moiré, halftones, which are grids of equally spaced dots, are angled at a nearly 30° difference between the strong colors. Usually, yellow is angled at a 15° difference from the strong colors. While making the halftone separations, the operator selects this angling so that films with the proper angles are output on the imagesetter or on the film plotter of a color scanner or color electronic prepress system (CEPS). Stochastic halftone screening[2] does not produce moiré and, therefore, does not have to be angled.

Production steps for good photomechanical color reproductions

1. Calibrate the scanner for the printing conditions, such as dot gain, ink and paper, and type of printing press or printer.
2. Modify the separations for the copy's characteristics and the customer's desires.
3. View the reproduction on a monitor calibrated to match the printed result.
4. Place the separations in an electronic page.
5. Produce the page as films on an imagesetter.
6. Proof the halftone separation films in such a way that the color proof matches the printed result.
7. Print on the press so that the press sheet matches the color proof.
8. Control the printing for hue consistency.

[2] *Stochastic halftone screening* uses algorithms to make halftones by varying the number of dots in an area to achieve differing tonal values. The dots are very small and all the same size. Some newer algorithms can also vary the dot sizes.

Conditions necessary for producing good color separations

To insure good color separations, the following conditions should be present:

- Memory colors of the correct hue, strength, and brightness,
- Contrast optimized for the printing conditions and the original,
- Color correction adjusted for the printing conditions, including the ink, paper, and original copy,
- Picture detail enhanced using unsharp masking to compensate for the scanner optics and the original photo,
- Color balance for overall good appearance.

The color separation process

Colored original copy that is chosen for reproduction may be a reflective photographic print, a color photographic transparency (a slide), artwork created on a substrate, or any object that can be scanned or photographed by a digital scanner or digital camera. The original is mounted on the scanner, which is either a flatbed or drum scanner. The color original is optically analyzed through colored filters. The scanner determines where, and how much, cyan, magenta and yellow will print in the reproduction. A light beam reflecting off the nontransparent original, or through the transparent original, passes through a red filter, a green filter and a blue filter to the optics. The red filter analyzes the cyan content of the original and is used to produce the cyan separation. The green filter analyzes the magenta content and is used to produce the magenta separation. The blue filter analyzes the yellow content and is used to produce the yellow separation. The scanner uses the signals from all three filters to make the black separation.

This data reflects the amounts of cyan, magenta and yellow present in all areas of the original copy and indicates the amount of ink on paper needed to recreate the original colors.

HIGHEND SCANNERS

How a highend scanner operates

In the worldwide graphic arts industry, the highend scanner has become the benchmark for all good color reproduction. Even though some desktop drum scanners and CCD scanners can almost match the quality of the highend scanner, it still makes the best separations. "Highend" refers to the price and the quality. Those in the printing industry know what it takes to produce good quality color on the printing press. Now, no matter how the separations are made, it's only a matter of adjusting the separations to the printing parameters.

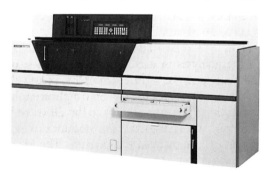

Figure 5 A typical highend color scanner

When running a highend scanner, the operator mounts the color transparency by taping it in position on a clear plastic cylinder or drum. The scanner analyzes the transparency point by point using light that shines first through the center of the drum and then through the transparency to the scanner optics. There the light splits into three beams that respectively pass through the red, the green and the blue filters. Information from the filters is used by the scanner to produce the four separations.

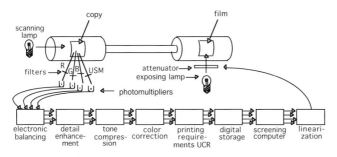

Figure 6 Simplified schematic of a basic color scanner

The scanner drum revolves at a high speed. During each revolution, the optics look at one row of information around that drum. Each row is made up of small spots called **pixels**. A pixel may vary from 1/100 of an inch to about one thousandth of an inch in diameter. During the analysis of each spot, before the scanner optics moves to the next spot, the light beam splits, passes through the red, green and blue filters and images onto a photomultiplier tube. The photomultiplier tubes are sensitive to the different light levels. The photomultiplier tubes measure the amount of red, green and blue light passing through from the original. The strength of the signals indicate the amount of cyan, magenta and yellow content in each spot of the original copy. A temporary scanner memory stores each row of pixel information. Each pixel in that row is recorded as one of 256 gray levels for each process color. At this point the color appears only as a level of gray. It no longer is a color.

The best way to visualize what the scanner sees is to look through a red filter at a colored picture. The red filter is red because only red

Figure 7 Gray levels of an image as it appears through a red filter

light passes through it. Since cyan absorbs red light, no light will pass through where cyan is in the copy. Therefore, you will see a darkness in the cyan area. The level of the darkness, which depends on the strength of the cyan, is recorded in the scanner pixel row memory. If you look though the green and blue filters at their complimentary colors of magenta and yellow, you will notice the same darkness in the magenta or yellow areas. The level of darkness for each is also recorded in the scanner pixel row memory.

As the cylinder revolves one revolution, the scanner samples the pixels around the drum, analyzes them and records a value for the cyan, magenta and yellow for each pixel. To compute the black amount needed in each pixel, the highend scanner analyzes the three values for each pixel. When all three signals (cyan, magenta and yellow) are heavy, there is quite a bit of black present. If only two are heavy, then the color is not black. It may be a saturated color. Therefore, the area needs no black or very little black.

After the cylinder has made one revolution, the scanner optics move over the width of one scan line, which is equal to the spot size. The cylinder makes the next revolution. The scanner repeats the process until the entire original image is scanned.

For film output, film is mounted on a separate revolving solid scanner drum. Exposing optics record the dot sizes necessary for the cyan, magenta, yellow and black halftone separations. With each revolution, one half a row of halftone dots is recorded. As a typical highend scanner analyzes and records each scan line, the scanner simultaneously records the previous scan line output onto the halftone film or stores the information on a magnetic disk. The scanner exposes or stores the images at the correct size for the finished color reproduction. Four halftone separation negatives or positives, ready for color proofing and manual stripping into a color page, are produced.

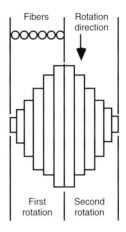

Figure 8 Halftone dot generation on film

Determining the needed scanner sampling rate

The final reproduction resolution determines the ***sampling rate***, or the number of pixels per inch scanned from an original. The ***resolution*** is the degree of detail in the output, in this case the separations. Unsharp masking, which is described later in this book, can enhance the image resolution, because it increases the edge sharpness. The resolution of input and output devices is often described by their rated pixels per inch or dots per inch (dpi).

Macintosh monitor .... 72 pixels per inch
Laser printers .... 300-1200 dpi
Imagesetters .... 1270-3386 dpi
Desktop scanners .... 300 to 6000 dpi
High-end scanners .... up to 10,000 dpi

In the graphic arts industry, it is customary to scan in two pixels for every halftone dot in both directions at the final size of the reproduction. These four pixels per dot are sufficient information to give the detail or resolution needed in the final reproduction. Most high-end scanners output films using two passes around the drum per row of halftone dots. That means for a same size reproduction using a 150 line screen, the scanner input scans at 300 pixels per inch,

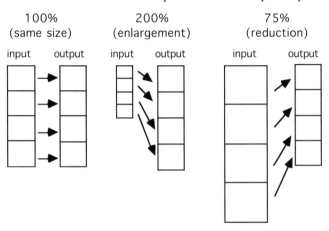

Figure 9   A 150 line screen enlargement on a highend scanner

which is equivalent to 300 lines per inch (lpi), to output 150 rows of dots per inch. Output requires two exposure passes to produce one row of dots, or 2.0 pixels per output halftone screen dot in each direction. The industry is moving toward using only 1.5 pixels per output halftone screen dot in each direction.

If the size of the reproduction differs from the size of the original, the operator sets the scanner to alter its input scanning rate as compared with its output scanning rate. The output exposure frequency is not changed; only the input scan frequency is modified. A reproduction that is twice as big in both directions as the original requires a 200 percent magnification. Using a 150 line screen output, the input is scanned in at 600 pixels and lines per inch frequency for 150 lines per inch output. There will have to be twice as many rows of dots as there would be for a 100 percent reproduction. When the reproduction enlargement size is entered during scanner setup, the scanner automatically increases the input scan frequency to produce the correct output size. When the pixels are output at normal scanner 300 lpi frequency for the 150 screen ruling, the reproduction will be the correct enlarged size. Enlarged highend scanner reproductions usually have better detail than enlarged CCD (charge-coupled device) scanner reproductions, because the highend scanner has the ability to increase the input sampling rate. If needed, the highend scanner takes many more samples from the same original. See How a desktop CCD color scanner works, page 22.

The more information the scanner obtains from the original during the scanning process, the larger the reproduction. Of course, the disadvantage of recording large amounts of original pixels is the large file size created. If you convert this large file to a Mac or PC file, the file size makes the task more difficult. To minimize file size and processing time, you should only scan for the anticipated reproduction size.

The general industry standard, "two pixels in both directions per halftone dot on the final size," always provides the full detail needed in the final reproduction. Some scanner operators have found that a resolution of only 1.5 pixels in both directions provides sufficient reproduction detail and smaller file sizes. In low frequency images, direct digital imaging technology can support as low as 1.2 pixels per output halftone screen dot in each direction. The files are only half, or even a fourth, as large as many industry experts might think necessary to produce a good-looking reproduction.

The amount of color picture data may cause the file size to become cumbersome. For example, a one square inch area screened for a 150 line halftone contains 22,500 dots per color. Multiplying 22,500 dots by four colors produces 90,000 dots. Multiplying 90,000 dots by four pixels per dot gives 360,000 pixels for a one square inch area. A 2 by 3 inch image contains 1.6 megabytes (Mb) for each file created. A 4 by 5 inch image contains 5.4 Mb. A full 8 by 10 inch page would contain 21.6 Mb for each file. Therefore, you can see why sampling at only 1.5 pixels or 1.2 pixels per halftone dot helps considerably to reduce the files size.

Questions are often asked about the differences between analog and digital scanners. It is interesting to note that all highend scanners are both analog and digital. That is, the original information is scanned in as analog data and converted to digital data. At some point in the color separation process, the scanner modifies the optical signal to a digital gray value, or gray level.

An *analog scanner* receives each light signal and converts the optical signal to an electrical signal of 0 to 10 volts. The scanner analyzes and processes the information as the voltages pass through built-in hard-wired circuits of resistors and transistors. Late in the scanning process, the analog scanner digitizes the information for storage in a temporary buffer. It holds a single row of pixel values for one revolution of the input cylinder before the data is output.

A *digital scanner* immediately digitizes the analyzed analog information from the photomultiplier tubes. This scanner processes the information digitally. This makes it possible to build algorithms for making the calculations in the software. The manipulated digital data is stored in a temporary buffer.

You can identify analog and digital scanners by observing their control panels. Analog scanners have many knobs for adjusting their circuits. Digital scanners usually have push button controls, rather than knobs. Both analog and digital scanners produce good quality color separations. However, the trend is away from analog scanners and toward digital scanners.

Analyzing the separations prior to making films

In the early days of scanning, it was not possible to view the scanned image prior to making the films. Scanner operators "flew by the seat of their pants" and hoped that they had done everything correctly for a good reproduction. Over the years, skilled operators learned what is needed to produce good reproductions. They could be confident in the results. Only after the analog color proof became available did the scanner operator and the customer know for sure that the separations would produce good reproductions. Before the digital color proof, the national average for getting an acceptable set of separations was three scans and three analog color proofs.

Today a highend scanner can be linked with a color electronic pre-press system or a desktop computer. Instead of sending the output pixel information to film, the scanner sends the entire four separations to a disk for digital storage. The digitally stored scanned image can be viewed on a monitor prior to making films. This not only permits anyone to view the scanned results, it facilitates either changing the scanned data to make a better image, or making the decision to rescan the image.

A color electronic prepress system (CEPS) is considered a highend retouching station. It has very high processing power and high throughput, as well as a high price tag. A CEPS allows the operator to view, retouch, modify and incorporate images into pages or flats for later output to page film, digital plates or gravure cylinders. The text for the pages is usually imported. Images from the CEPS can be archived to magnetic disks, optical discs or data tapes.

Currently equipment manufacturers are trying to help the desktop computer catch up with the CEPS in functionality, processing power and throughput. While not there yet, the Mac and the PC offer a tremendous advantage over just having a highend scanner. With the desktop computer, it is possible to electronically make separations, view, retouch, modify and incorporate images into digital pages that can also be corrected and modified as needed. This is not possible using highend scanners alone.

DESKTOP SCANNERS

Desktop drum scanners vs. highend scanners

When desktop drum color scanners are compared to highend scanners, the following differences and similarities are found. The desktop drum scanners:

- are much lower in cost than the highend scanners.
- try to emulate highend scanners. Their revolving drum and photomultiplier tubes analyze and capture the original image.
- function in much the same way as highend scanners. However, most desktop drum scanners do not carry out all the highend scanner functions.
- may give only red, green and blue (RGB) signal digital output. They may not be able to convert from RGB signals to CMYK (cyan, magenta, yellow and black) as a highend scanner does on the fly. The computer's separation software will convert the image to CMYK. You can avoid the transformation problems if you can work in CMYK from the start.
- may require the use of a computer and software to do color correction or unsharp masking after the original image has been scanned. The highend scanner does this on the fly, as it makes the separation and outputs the data.
- can be programmed and operated from the desktop computer to do multiple scans in an automatic mode without operator intervention. This is not possible with most highend scanners.
- cannot produce film directly like highend scanners do; an imagesetter is needed for film output.

Desktop drum scanner costs

Desktop drum scanners are considered midrange scanners. Currently, they are available from such manufacturers as Howtek, Dainippon Screen, Optronics, Damark and others. There are over 50 manufacturers of all types of scanners. In 1993, midrange desktop drum scanners cost anywhere from 10,000-60,000 U.S. dollars depending on the sophistication of the scanner and the options.

Figure 10 Typical desktop drum scanner

Most desktop drum scanners are controlled remotely from the Mac or PC. Preprogrammed from the desktop computer for each original mounted on the drum, the scanner scans each original, one after another, without operator intervention. This kind of operation is very cost-effective.

Compared with the highend scanner, the operation of the desktop drum scanner is relatively easy. This eliminates the cost and training time investments that are needed to become a highend scanner operator. A desktop scanner operator learns in a short time. Most guesswork is eliminated because the scans are made, and later adjusted visually for the printing conditions, based on the computer monitor image. Today's desktop color separation software

Screen DS-608
highend color scanner with
on-the-fly USM, color correction and CMYK output

Optronics ColorGetter
desktop color drum
scanner

Scitex Smart Scanner PS
Image captured and cus-
tomized with the Scitex
software

Figure 11A Comparison of scans from different input color scanners

Howtek D-4000 desktop
color drum scanner

Agfa Horizon desktop
flatbed color scanner

Kodak Photo CD 35mm
color scanner
Image obtained with Kodak
Acquire Photoshop plug-in
extension

Figure 11B Comparison of scans from different input color scanners

facilitates the data adjustment for good color. "What you see is what you can expect to get in the reproduction."

How a desktop CCD color scanner works

Generally, a CCD (charge-coupled device) color separation scanner is a flatbed device. The operator places the original reflection or transparent copy on a flat glass surface for color analysis. During the color analysis of the original, the light beam reflects from the original or transmits through the original to the photodetectors

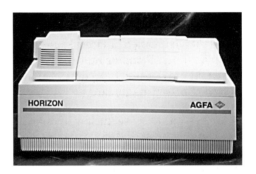

Figure 12 Typical desktop CCD scanner

known as **CCDs**. These miniature sensors are arranged in a two-inch long, straight line on a computer chip called a **CCD array**. This CCD array may contain as many as 2000 sensors in the two-inch space. The CCD scanner may have one linear CCD array with filters that rotate over the CCD array to obtain the red, green and blue image. Or, more sophisticated desktop CCD color scanners have three parallel linear CCD arrays, one with a red filter, one with a green filter and one with a blue filter.

A desktop CCD color scanner analyzes the original by imaging the width of the picture over the length of its CCD array. Therefore, if the CCD array contains 2000 sensors, regardless of the width of the picture, a maximum of 2000 pixels are recorded across the width dimension. In a desktop CCD color scanner the original moves sideways over the stationary CCD array. As the original moves one width of the array, a snapshot is taken of each line of the original. When the entire picture is digitized and stored, either in the computer RAM or on a disk, the process is complete. If the scanner has three CCD arrays, the scan time is much faster than if the scanner requires a separate and successive red scan, green scan and blue scan of the original.

Highend and desktop drum separations vs. CCD separations

Generally, CCDs (charge-coupled devices) have less dynamic range than photomultiplier tubes. ***Dynamic range*** is the range between the minimum and maximum density. In an optical imaging device, it is a measure of the device's sensitivity range (more details on page 32).

CCD scanners are not able to sense the low light level differences in the dark shadow areas as well as desktop drum and highend scanners. This inability may cause the reproduction to have less detail and less color separation in the dark shadow areas than highend or desktop drum separations have.

The desktop CCD scanner resolution is more limited than highend or desktop drum scanner resolution. To change the desktop drum scanner reproduction sizes, the captured image data is mathematically adjusted. The amount of information already captured is either compressed or enlarged. With the CCD scanner, the amount of pixel information gathered is the same regardless of the original's size. If the number of CCD cells are sufficient to capture enough information for two pixels per dot across the image, then there will be no difficulty reproducing the original. However, to enlarge the reproduction, there may be a visible degradation of the image quality. This is because there will be less than two pixels per halftone dot in both directions. In some cases, 1.5 pixels or 1.2 pixels per halftone dot in each direction are sufficient.

Compared to the highend scanner, another CCD scanner disadvantage is that it generally cannot do unsharp masking or color correction on the fly. These two functions must be done after the scan is finished, using a PC or Mac and available software, and the stored digital information. This increases the throughput time.

DIGITAL STILL PHOTOGRAPHY

The digital still camera is becoming a very popular method of capturing images in a digital RGB color space for later use in color reproduction. Because the image is already in digital form, production costs and throughput time are reduced. No film originals are necessary, and fewer steps are needed for color reproduction. Also, the photographer has an instant image with which to check the photographic results.

Each new camera generation has improved image resolution. Currently it is not as high as photographic film or most color scanners. If you expect to keep the pixel to dot ratio of 2 to 1, the resolution limits the size of magnification possible. However, a digital camera does not have grain-like film. Therefore, the image can be mathematically enlarged by using fewer than two pixels per dot. The pixel to dot ratio can be reduced to 1 to 1, utilizing unsharp masking techniques to maintain image sharpness. While this does not create image detail that isn't in the original image, it does permit larger reproductions from digitally captured images.

As with other scanned images, digital photographic images must be modified for the printing conditions and customer's desires. This is done on the Mac or PC after photography and before page assembly.

KODAK PHOTO CD SYSTEM

How the Kodak Photo CD system operates

The Kodak Photo CD system uses a CCD scanner that scans in the original information at a 2,000 line per inch resolution with 12 bits per color. Kodak personnel determined that this scanning resolution will capture enough data to enlarge a 35 mm film image to a 16 by 20 inch color print with sufficient detail to equal an optically enlarged print. The RGB information for the entire 35 mm transparency is captured in a six second scan. The Pro Model scanner handles 4 by 5 inch copy and scans the original at 4,000 lines per inch on input.

Information is saved in the Kodak YCC color space format relative to the original scene rather than relative to the transparency. The RGB information is converted to luminance and chrominance. Y represents levels of brightness in luminance. CC values represent the hue in terms of chrominance. The color transforms used permit a color gamut large enough to support any color device. Each stored image is color balanced and adjusted for exposure. Therefore, originals with different characteristics can be used side by side in a final reproduction.

Using a prescan, a built-in algorithm returns the transparency's appearance to the appearance of the original scene. It adjusts the scene automatically to compensate for the original exposure and the film type that was used to capture the image. The software subtracts the characteristics of the film used. This makes the film type and film speed immaterial. It does not matter whether the original is negative, positive, Kodachrome, Ektachrome, Fujichrome or

Agfachrome. Regardless of the film used, a reproduction identical to the original scene will be produced. This is a unique feature. It does not make images ready for printing. They still need the same image adjustments that other scans require.

There has been some rethinking of the desire to automatically return the reproduction's appearance to the original scene's color appearance. Most graphic arts people attempt to reproduce the original transparency's appearance, rather than the appearance of the original scene before it was captured. This also may be desirable for Photo CD images. Therefore the automatic function can be turned off, so that the reproduction will be more accurate to the visual appearance of the scanned-in original.

Using the Kodak Photo CD system still requires that you customize the images for your printing conditions and the customer's desires. The Kodak algorithms cannot prepare the files for specific printing conditions because the system has no way of knowing what they are. Adjustments for contrast, color correction and USM (unsharp masking) are still required.

Image storage and retrieval

The images are stored on a *CD (compact disc)*. This CD is similar in size and appearance to the disc used in your audio system. However, standard audio CD format is different from Photo CD format. It can only be read by compatible Photo CD ROM drives.

A consideration when buying a Photo CD ROM drive is whether or not it is a multi-session drive. A "session" is generally the placement of digitized images from one roll of film on the Photo CD disc. Add more images later, and it becomes a multi-session disc. Only multi-session drives can access multi-session discs.

The processed image captured by the Photo CD scanner is stored in the Kodak YCC color space format. A 35 mm transparency scan generates 18 megabytes (Mb) of information in an uncompressed format. A clever system of subsampling, image recomposition and data compression makes it possible to store as many as 100 images on a single disc. Only 6 megabytes of information per image are required with lossless compression. **Lossless compression** means that there is no loss of data during the data compression. This is contrasted with **lossy compression** where a high compression rate is achieved by sacrificing an acceptable amount of data.

Images can be retrieved from the CD ROM at different resolutions. Which resolution is chosen is determined by the size of the reproduction's enlargement. A unique hierarchical image encoding scheme facilitates image retrieval. High resolution components are compressed and decomposed for efficient storage. To provide quicker monitor access, low resolution images are not compressed. While current CD ROM devices read at about 150 kilobytes per second (Kbs), new drives will read two to four times faster. Still, image retrieval time is an issue.

Image Pack

An **Image Pack** is the name given to all the image resolution components for one image on a disc. With a single high resolution scan of the 35 mm film to a Photo CD, there are five resolutions available. The process of creating these resolutions from a single scan is called a spatial decomposition. The five Photo CD image components and resolutions after image recomposition are shown in Figure 13.

Note that the scan done by the scanner is the highest resolution file, 16Base. This image is always available for retrieval. Uncompressed, the information alone would be 18 Mb. The Base/16 file is used for index files, icons and thumbnail images.

The Base (768 pixels by 512 lines) file is stored at the correct resolution for display on a TV monitor.

The 16Base scanned 18 Mb image is decomposed to provide the lower resolution files. The three highest resolutions are recorded to the Base image in a non-redundant fashion. A special method of encoding the images records only the differences between the higher and lower resolutions. The highest resolution file is mathematically decomposed to a 4Base and then to a Base file of 1.18 Mb,

Base	Pixel resolution	File size
Base/16	192 pixels by 128 lines	24,576 K
Base/4	384 pixels by 256 lines	98,304 K
Base	768 pixels by 512 lines	1.18 Mb
4Base	1536 pixels by 1024 lines	4.7 Mb
16Base	3072 pixels by 2048 lines	18.8 Mb

Figure 13 The five Photo CD image components and resolutions after image recomposition

which is saved. The Base image is the same resolution as the TV or computer monitor. This shortens the display time. The 4Base image is mathematically reconstructed from the Base image. The original 4Base file and the newly reconstructed 4Base file are compared. The difference is computed. This difference is called a residual and is stored in a compressed format. The same technique is used for the 16Base file. Therefore, by storing only the Base 1.18 Mb file, the residuals, and the lower Base/4 and Base/16 files, you can reconstruct both high resolution images and only require about 6 Mb of storage per image. There is no apparent loss of resolution.

Choosing a resolution

Your choice of resolution and file size will be determined by the reproduction's enlargement size. Reproductions that are larger than 800 percent may not contain sufficient detail. When making enlargements of this size, it would be better to use a desktop drum scanner or a highend scanner. Suggested resolutions for different sized reproductions, when the original is a 35 mm transparency, are shown in Figure 14.

Reproduction size	Resolution	File size
1 - 3 inch	Base	1.18 Mb
4 - 6 inch	4Base	4.7 Mb
7 - 10 inch	16Base	18.8 Mb
Larger sizes		
not recommended		

Figure 14 Suggested resolutions for different sized reproductions, when the original is a 35 mm transparency

Kodak Photo CD system advantages

The Kodak Photo CD system allows you to make up pages without having to operate or purchase a color scanner. For a low cost investment, you can purchase a Photo CD ROM drive and computer software that allows you to do your own prepress. The scans are captured directly from your photographs, either negatives or transparencies, and input to a CD ROM. The photofinisher or the service bureau does these scans for only a few dollars each. A disc holds as many as 100 images. You then have many scanned images including the high-resolution images for reproduction, the stored resolution view files and the thumbnail image for file management.

OBTAINING THE BEST POSSIBLE COLOR REPRODUCTIONS

Choosing the color film for capturing original images

If you have any influence with your photographers, suggest that they use the slowest possible film speed when capturing images for reproduction. Slower film speeds produce finer grained images. The faster the film speeds are, the grainier the images. Today, color negative films can be scanned on most color scanners. Color negative films usually have very fine grain. If large posters or very large format reproductions are being made, your photographer should use a film format larger than 35 mm. Two and a quarter inch square, a 120 mm film format or four by five inch film format will make the best large reproductions. Large format films result in large reproductions that have better resolution and less graininess.

Choosing a scanner

The scanner you select influences your image quality, your productivity and your throughput. A highend scanner generally produces the best quality reproduction. A midrange, desktop drum scanner yields the next best quality level. Generally, the CCD scanner produces the lowest quality reproduction image. However, with today's technology, the separation quality difference among the three scanner types is very small. The lower cost scanners are continuing to improve in terms of quality and throughput speed.

Linking a highend scanner to a Mac or PC

The highend scanner linked to your PC or Mac is the best configuration for quality and productivity. This combination enables you to first capture a highend scan. Then, using your PC or Mac, you can modify the scans in a manner similar to that normally done on an expensive CEPS. If you link your highend scanner to your Mac or PC, you gain the following:

- high quality images with a fast throughput,
- tone reproduction, color correction and unsharp masking on the fly,
- retouching and image modification on the Macintosh or PC,
- page makeup and retouching that are less expensive than the same tasks accomplished on a CEPS, and
- control over the page because you do it yourself.

Optimizing the color scans

Regardless of which scanner you use to capture the images, the separation quality is going to depend on your ability to optimize the color scans for your printing conditions, the original's characteristics and the desires of the customer. It will require the following adjustments:

- contrast
- color correction
- detail enhancement using unsharp masking
- gray balance, and
- color balance.

The importance of contrast for optimum color

Contrast, the most important attribute for optimum color, is the difference between the whitest white and the blackest black. Also called *tone reproduction* and *gradation*, contrast is influenced significantly by the density range achievable for a given set of printing conditions. *Density range*, also called *dynamic range*, is the mathematical difference between the lightest and darkest tones as measured with a densitometer. For example, on an original transparency a 0.25 highlight density subtracted from a 3.0 shadow density would result in a 2.75 density range. On the desktop, you don't have to know the exact densities to make the separation setup.

The highest contrast printed image is possible on coated paper. A glossy surface produces darker shadows and brighter highlights than other paper types. A four-color density of 2.00 is achievable on coated paper printed on sheetfed commercial presses. Coated paper printed web offset using SWOP (Specification for Web Offset Publications), such as magazine publications, produces a density range equal to coated paper printed sheetfed. It is possible to get a 1.9 to 2.0 shadow density on coated paper printed web offset. Subtracting the 0.10 paper highlight density from the 2.00 shadow density, 1.9 is the resulting density range.

Using SNAP (Specifications for Non-Heat Advertising Printing) and printing by web offset on newsprint paper, such as your local newspaper, a four-color shadow density of only 1.40 is achievable. Subtracting the 0.20 highlight density of the paper only gives a 1.20 density range. Gravure and flexographic printing have the same density range as lithography for each appropriate paper type.

The secret to producing good color reproductions is adjusting the tone reproduction to achieve the proper tone compression for a given printing condition and original. *Tone compression* is the reduction of an original's tonal range to one that is achievable using the reproduction process. This is usually necessary, because most original copy's density range is greater than that of the printed reproduction. A transparency used as original copy usually has a 2.60 density range from the highlight to the shadow areas. Reflection copy may have a 2.00 density range.

Ideal contrast for clean, bright colors

An ideal color reproduction might be an exact copy of the original. When a comparison of each original density to each reproduced density is plotted, the ideal color reproduction's contrast, or tone reproduction, would be a 45° line if it were drawn on a graph similar to the one used in Figure 15. However, in actual practice, when the contrast of most reproductions is plotted, it is slightly lower than a 45° line and looks like the "S" shaped curve in the same illustration.

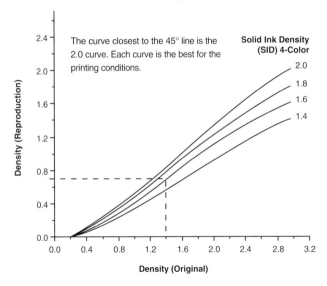

Figure 15 Tone reproduction plots comparing input and output densities that produce ideal reproductions for different printing conditions

For each paper and printing process, the exact shape of the ideal curve needs to be determined. Usually the contrast must be adjusted to keep the highlight clean and neutral white, the shadows dark, and the middletone clean and not too dark.

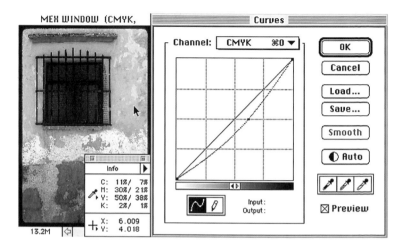

Figure 16 Tone reproduction plot of a gray scale after image modification in Photoshop curves on the Mac or PC

While observing the image on a color monitor and using appropriate software, you can visually modify the image to achieve the best possible reproduction for a given set of printing conditions. The highlight, shadow and middletone dot sizes are adjusted. If you were to plot the resulting gray scales,[3] you could expect to get one of the curves shown in Figure 17.

---

[3] *A gray scale* is a tone scale, a strip of gray patches or steps ranging from white to black in either varying densities or varying dot sizes from 0% to 100%. It is used to analyze printing characteristics. It may be made on photographic paper, on a strip of film, on a color proof or printed on paper. On a computer monitor, shades of gray are created by varying the apparent intensity of the screen's pixels, rather than by using a combination of only black-and-white pixels to produce shading. The densities of the steps represent the densities found in the image.

The paper and ink, dot gain, dot sizes, color correction, the printing sequence, gray balance and unsharp masking (USM) are all variables that affect the printed reproduction. If you understand the effect that each variable has on your results, then it is easier to adjust your separations for the printing conditions, the original characteristics and the customer's desires. In the following sections these variables will all be considered.

The effect of paper and ink on contrast (tone reproduction)

The effect of paper on the printing contrast is shown on the graph in Figure 17. Densities are compared by plotting the original densities

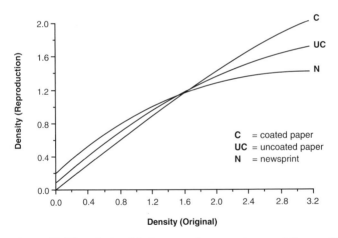

Figure 17 The relationship between the paper type and the resulting solid ink densities and gray scales produced using the same printing and inking conditions

along the x axis and the reproduction densities on the y axis. When a reproduction is analyzed, every original density is compared to every reproduction density. Analysis of a perfect reproduction results in a 45° straight line. In most cases, printing different solid ink densities (SIDs) results in "S" shaped curved lines for different paper types. Figure 17 illustrates how coated paper (C), uncoated paper (UC) and newsprint (N) affect the contrast.

Reproductions on coated paper have the highest contrast. Reproductions on uncoated paper have lower contrast, and reproductions on newsprint have the lowest contrast. On newsprint, the curve is very flat in the shadows. *Flat* describes low contrast pictures. This descriptive term came from the appearance of this curve. Flat means that either there is little or no difference in shadow densities, or if the original had detail, there's no longer any in the reproduction. Proper adjustment of the density range for different printing conditions produces the best possible contrast and results in a plotted line on the graph that is close to the ideal printed density range curve (see Figure 15).

Dot gain and its effect on the reproduction

During the printing process, dot gain is the most important variable to control. *Dot gain* is the increase in the apparent, measured dot size from the separation film to the printed reproduction. It is the physical enlargement of the dot caused by plate exposure image spread, by the pressures between the plate blanket and impression cylinder of a press, or by ink spread as it penetrates the paper.

The dot gain can be 5% to 35% depending on the amount of ink applied and the kind of paper. Usually, lower quality papers produce higher dot gain. Dot gain causes middletone image darkening because of the apparent dot increase in optical and physical size. Most dot gain is an optical gain. Light is trapped under the edges of printed dots. Because of this border zone effect, the dots with the largest circumference gain the most. Those are usually the 50 percent dot sizes. Border zone effect also explains why finer screen rulings have higher dot gain. Finer screen rulings have more dots per inch to grow. There is no way to change this phenomenon. However, to compensate for the problem, the separations can be adjusted when they are made. If a 20% dot gain is expected, then the dot sizes on the films can be reduced 20% to compensate for what will happen during the printing process.

An isoconture curve such as the one plotted in Figure 18 shows the typical effect of dot gain from the zero to 100% dot size on the film.

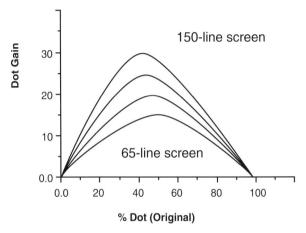

Figure 18   Isoconture curves showing the typical dot gain from the film to the printed dots, including the optical dot gain

Dot gain is measured in the middletone patch, because the majority of dot gain takes place in the middletones. The higher the dot gain, the higher the middletone density will appear.

Consider the magenta printer. The same halftone separation films printed on different presses using different papers can produce different dot gain percents that range from acceptable to totally unacceptable. Therefore, the dot gain effect on the halftone's contrast varies. Before making the films the separator needs to know what type of press and paper will be used.

On the graph in Figure 19, observe what happens to the curve when the magenta solid ink density (SID), or amount of magenta ink, is increased. As it increases, the shadow density increases. However, the middletones gain density more quickly than the shadows. The increased middletone dot gain lowers the shadow contrast. This results in a picture that no longer appears sharp and attractive. Often such a picture is described as being plugged up. ***Plugged up*** describes the phenomena of ink printing in the white spaces between the dots. As the dots increase in size, the spaces fill in and the dots begin printing on top of other printed dots. The amount of ink being printed could be reduced. However, enough ink must be printed to achieve saturated colors. To get the best possible reproduction, a compromise is necessary between the amount of ink put on the paper and how much dot gain you will accept.

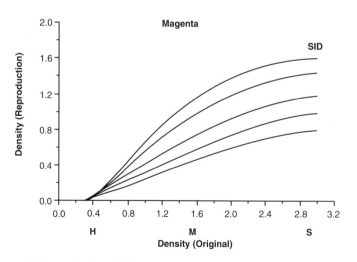

Figure 19 Graph demonstrating how the middletone densities are increased when the ink amount is increased

In Figure 20, look at the curve comparing the densities of the original to the reproduction's percent dot area. Note that the center line represents the desired screening curve. The two curves above this line represent how dot gain affects the reproduction's printed dot areas.

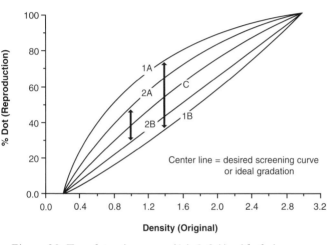

Figure 20 Two dot gain curves (1A & 2A) with their corresponding middletone reduction (1B & 2B) to produce the ideal gradation (C)

The question is: How do you compensate and make the curves more like the desired curve?

The answer is: You adjust the middletone of the curve below the center line by an equal amount to that above the center line, so that the result is a line more like the desired screening curve. This is accomplished by reducing the middletone dot sizes. If there will be a 10% dot gain, reduce the middletone by 10%. For a 20% dot gain, reduce the middletone by 20%. Therefore, the secret to good color reproduction is reducing the middletone dot sizes for the printing conditions (the press and paper).

Studies have been done to determine the average "fingerprint" of most printing presses. Thousands of presses have been thoroughly analyzed. The studies showed that there is quite a bit of press variation. However, when the industry averages are known, people tend to work toward those averages. Today, the industry aims for the middle of the dot gain variation. If separations are made that fit that value, the separations will accommodate the given printing

Figure 21A This reproduction is printed on a coated paper and appears bright

Figure 21B A simulation of the same image printed on uncoated paper using the same films

conditions. Refer to the information in Figure 22. It shows ideal halftone screening dot sizes for separation films for the three basic printing conditions. These guidelines should produce good reproductions. Whether you are using coated paper sheetfed, coated paper webfed, uncoated paper sheetfed, or newsprint webfed, these are the default settings that you will use to adjust your separations for those printing conditions. Use them for the setup profiles and preferences. The default settings for coated paper webfed and uncoated paper sheetfed are the same. Newsprint is almost always printed on a web press.

Coated paper sheetfed

Original	Cyan	Magenta	Yellow	Black
H 0.30	7	5	5	0
M 1.30	62	50	50	22
S 2.90	97	90	90	80

Coated paper webfed (SWOP) or uncoated paper sheetfed

Original	Cyan	Magenta	Yellow	Black
H 0.30	5	3	3	0
M 1.30	52	40	40	18
S 2.90	95	85	85	75
S GCR	75	65	65	95

Newsprint paper webfed (SNAP)

Original	Cyan	Magenta	Yellow	Black
H 0.30	3	1	1	0
M 1.30	42	30	30	15
S 2.90	92	82	82	70
S GCR	72	62	62	90

GCR = gray component replacement (See page 59, footnote 6)

Figure 22   A chart showing ideal halftone screening dot sizes for separation films

Using the densitometer function

Critical to your color success is the accurate contrast adjustment of the color separation image. It is not always easy to exactly determine what dot size you have in any image area by looking at the monitor screen. The computer application software has a densitometer function. By activating this function, you can automatically take dot areas readings for each of the four separations. You simply click on any area in the image and the dot size appears on the screen. By so doing, you can compare these readings to those you expect for gray balance or a color in any part of the tone scale.

The densitometer readings for dot area indicate dot area in the film, not what will be printed. Since all printing conditions are different, you must rely on the dot areas on the films as your reference. Into the application's preferences, you must input the expected dot gain for your chosen printing system. Then, the video display should give you an accurate representation of the expected printed image.

With your computer software application, you can also check exact color specifications to determine how any given color hue and strength will appear printed. By making a dot area measurement on the monitor's image, you can compare these results with those given in a color tint book or fan book. Such books are produced by TRUMATCH, Pantone, Focaltone and Agfa Division of Miles Corporation. The appearance of the book's printed swatches indicates what you can expect on your paper with your chosen printing method. This color comparison technique is called *swatching out* a color. Be sure to use the paper type that matches your paper.

Adjusting the separation contrast to the copy

The copy is another variation in the separation process. Based on the information in Figure 22, you should set your preferences in the computer for your printing conditions. These settings will produce good separations, provided you fit them to your copy characteristics. Every original copy has unique highlight, shadow and middletone densities. Every original copy also has a particular distribution of the densities between the highlight and shadow, known as its *keyness*.[4] This density distribution is determined by the copy image content. Some original copy has an unwanted color cast.[5] You must modify the contrast for copy attributes, such as keyness and color casts. These adjustments are important and will most likely determine whether or not you produce a good quality color reproduction.

When adjusting the computer for separation contrast, the *highlight dot placement* is usually the first setting made. After the scanned digital image is imported, you determine where the highlights are in the original image and what are the correct highlight dot sizes for the cyan, magenta, yellow and black separations. This is accomplished by whatever technique your software recommends. It may be as simple as first clicking on the highlight icon and then clicking on the highlight position in the copy.

The highlight dot sizes are placed in the *diffuse highlights*. These are the whitest parts of the picture that have detail and are neutral white. Placing the highlight dots in the correct image areas insures that the diffuse highlights are neutral white and will have detail in the reproduction. *Specular highlights*, such as the reflections on silverware or glassware, should not have dots printing in them. If they do, this is a clue that you have misplaced the highlight dots.

Second, the *shadow dot placement* is determined. The shadow dots should be placed in the darkest part of the picture image. Again it simply may be a matter of first clicking on a shadow icon and then on the shadow portion of the image. The shadow should be a neutral black that has no color. When a transparency is used as original

---

[4] *Keyness* describes the tonal values in a picture. It is the distribution of the densities between the highlight and shadow. If the picture has mostly highlights, it is labeled "high key." If the picture is predominately dark areas, it is called "low key." If the picture has equal amounts of highlights, middletones and shadows, it is described as "normal key."

[5] *Color cast* is an unwanted overall discoloration, or color tinting, of the original, the color proof or the reproduction by the trace of some color hue. A color cast results in colors that are too blue, green or red. Color comparisons between the original, computer screen image, color proof, and press sheets should always be done in standard lighting, 5000K color temperature, because the color of the light source will affect color appearance. During or following scanning, the color cast can be digitally altered or removed. Color casts are also referred to as color biases and color shifts.

Small highlight dots do not carry any highlight detail in the diffuse highlight areas. Such dots may be required when printing on darker papers, such as newsprint, because larger highlight dots may dirty up some of the colors.

Normal highlight dots put the minimum dot sizes in the diffuse highlight areas, giving neutral white detail. There should be no dots in specular highlights. Dot sizes depend on the paper type. Larger highlight dot sizes are possible on coated paper.

Large highlight dots darken the picture and begin to put too much of the wrong colors in the wrong places. If dots are printing in the specular highlights, this is a sign that the highlight dots are too large for the conditions.

Figure 23 Highlight dot placement

Too small shadow dot sizes lower the reproduction's contrast. The very dark shadows of the original will not reproduce. To adjust for the original's density range, the shadow must be placed in the shadow areas of the picture.

Normal shadow dot sizes placed in the correct shadow areas of the original produce a pleasing color reproduction. When the two are compared visually, the reproduction has the same neutral black shadow detail as the original.

Too large shadow dot sizes cause too much of all colors to print in the dark areas, and many of the saturated colors may become the wrong color. Placed too close to the highlights, too large shadow dots darken the reproduction and begin to dirty up the colors.

Figure 24 Shadow dot placement

copy, and there are no appropriate dark shadows in the image, it sometimes is necessary to place the shadow dots within the border of the image.

After the highlight dot placement and shadow dot placement has been determined, you next adjust your ***printing density range*** to fit your copy density range. This insures that the maximum possible contrast will be achieved. It also minimizes any color cast the copy may have had in the highlight or shadow. The values in the table, Figure 22, produce neutral gray in the highlights, middletones and shadows. The assumption is that if the tone reproduction curves are adjusted properly, the three aim-points will also produce neutral grays in all steps of the gray scale. The mere fact that you place the highlight and shadow according to these guidelines insures neutral grays in all gray areas of the reproduction.

Adjusting the middletone contrast for the copy keyness

An original with evenly distributed densities over the tonal scale is considered *normal key*. An original that has most of its important detail in the highlight areas is called *high key*. An original that has most of its detail in the darker shadows is called *low key*.

The middletone dot sizes are adjusted to get the most pleasing reproduction. Usually it is advantageous to not only adjust the middletone for the printing conditions, but also to achieve the higher contrast in the important detail areas of the picture. Making this adjustment while observing the image on a computer monitor enables the operator to see what the reproduction will look like when printed. The middletones can be moved up or down the tone scale. An almost instant outcome can be observed on the monitor screen. By trial and error, the operator can lighten or darken the reproduction to get the desired effect.

Darkening the middletone puts more contrast in the highlight areas and lowers the shadow contrast. The shadows become dark and the contrast flat. Conversely, lightening the middletones will put more contrast in the shadow areas and will flatten out the highlight contrast. By lightening or darkening the middletone portion of the cyan, magenta, yellow and black curves together while keeping the gray balance, the operator can keep the correct color balance, even though the contrast has changed. These middletone changes can be used to add detail in important parts of the reproduction. They also can be used to satisfy customer requests for such things as "opening up the shadows," or "cleaning up the colors."

Clean and bright or dull and gray

The highlight, shadow and middletone dot placements in the picture determine whether or not you satisfy the customer and get the best possible color reproduction. If the highlight, shadow and middletone dots are not first adjusted correctly, any other adjustments that you make will only produce minor differences. Other modifications will not correct for an improper contrast adjustment. Adjusting the contrast accurately by modifying the highlight, shadow and middletone dots correctly is the most important thing you will do to produce a customer-satisfying, good reproduction.

Improper contrast, or tone reproduction, adjustment puts the wrong colors in the wrong places in the reproduction. For example, if too much middletone dot is printing, too much cyan will print in reds, too much magenta in green grass and too much yellow in blue skies. The colors will be dirty. The effect is the same as printing too much black in the colored areas. It darkens the picture and muddies up the colors.

Keeping the middletones where they should be, or a little lighter than they should be, facilitates good color reproductions on press

Sheetfed litho on coated paper has the lowest percentage dot gain. To compensate for dot gain darkening, the middletone dot sizes are reduced. Typical dot sizes are cyan 62%, magenta and yellow 50%, and black 22%.

Web offset on coated or **sheetfed on uncoated** have more dot gain than sheetfed litho on coated paper. Also, to gain shadow detail, the middle tones may need to be lightened. Typical middletone dot sizes are cyan 52%, magenta and yellow 40%, and black 18%.

Web offset on newsprint gains 25-35%. This dot gain, plus the darker paper, decreases shadow contrast and darkens the color reproduction. Typical middletone dot sizes are cyan 42%, magenta and yellow 30%, and black 15%.

Figure 25 Middletone dot placement

and cleans up colors, making them brighter. When the highlights, shadows and middletones are correct, only minor additional corrections are needed to produce good color reproductions. Makeready is shorter on press. Color OKs are easier. Customers are happier. The printed results are more likely to look like the color proof.

> *The worst mistake that you can make is putting too much printing dot in the middletones.*

The Scitex Smart™ Scanner, a CCD input device, has built-in algorithms that automatically evaluate the original during a prescan and adjust the highlight, middletone and shadow dot sizes for each original subject for the given printing conditions. This scanner automatically does what highend scanner operators do and what Mac and PC users can do with specialized software. The latest models of highend scanners can also use artificial intelligence to automatically set the highlight and shadow points. If you are not using software, on your Mac or PC, that adjusts the highlight, middletone and shadow dot sizes for each original subject and the given printing conditions, then you need to take advantage of the graphic arts industry's knowledge about dot size placement and use the correct values in your desktop separations (See *Figure 22 A chart showing ideal halftone screening dot sizes for separation films*).

Color correction

Not-so-perfect process inks make color correction necessary. The process cyan ink used by most printing processes appears as if it has too much magenta and yellow pigment. As much as a 25% hue error may be present. Magenta inks also have a serious hue error.

Magenta inks have too much yellow pigment—sometimes as much as a 45% hue error. The yellow ink is the most pure ink. However, it is contaminated with a small amount of magenta, about 10%.

Every color scanner, or its accompanying software, must somehow compensate for the printing inks.

Looking at the ink appearance representations in Figure 26, you will notice that the extra magenta and yellow make all three inks appear to have orange in them. You compensate for the contaminated inks using the algorithms built into the scanner or computer software. The algorithms selectively reduce the magenta dot sizes where magenta prints with cyan. Printing smaller magenta dot sizes with cyan compensates for the extra magenta contamination in the cyan ink. This keeps blues from becoming purple. To prevent the reds from being orange, yellow is reduced where it prints with magenta. Also, magenta is slightly decreased in areas where yellow prints.

$$C = C_{+M+Y} \qquad\qquad C = \text{cyan}$$
$$M = M_{+Y} \qquad\qquad M = \text{magenta}$$
$$Y = Y_{+M} \qquad\qquad Y = \text{yellow}$$

Figure 26 Appearance of inks with the extra magenta and yellow

Selective color corrections can change the hue and strength of all the cyan, magenta, yellow, red, green and blue in a color image. In Adobe Photoshop, the hue and saturation control under Image-Adjust would be used to make any selective color modifications.

The operator may have to fine-tune the color correction software for each ink set. In addition, slight modifications can be made for small ink trapping differences. ***Ink trapping*** is the ability of one wet ink to stick over another wet ink. One hundred percent trapping occurs when the same amount of ink prints on top of the first ink as prints on the unprinted surface. More often, undertrapping occurs. One wet ink will not adhere properly when it is applied over another wet ink. Ink trapping should not be confused with image trapping. *Image trapping* is the overlapping of different color image edges to minimize the effect of misregister and to prevent a white line appearing between two color images during the printing process.

Printing sequence

The printing sequence affects color quality. Today the most common worldwide printing sequence is black, cyan, magenta and yellow, KCMY. Changing this printing sequence may have a slight effect on the ink trapping and the amount of color correction needed. The color correction may have to be fine-tuned by the computer operator. In most cases, color correction is set up as a default condition. Once adjusted, it is left alone.

Selective color corrections, or minor corrections in certain areas of the picture, are possible. Using a computer retouching program, you may make editorial color changes. In some cases, the customer desires a color change. In other cases, unique printing conditions make it necessary.

Determining gray balance

Gray balance is a necessary attribute of good color reproduction. It is reproducing any neutral gray in the original as a gray in the reproduction. The proper amount of cyan, magenta and yellow must print to produce a gray scale with no apparent dominant hue. The extra magenta and yellow in process inks tend to produce a brown rather than a neutral gray scale. Figure 27 illustrates three different gray scales, two that are non-neutral.

To reproduce neutral grays, you must compensate for the ink contamination. The magenta ink and yellow ink dot sizes are reduced throughout the printing scale, in neutral gray areas, from the highlight to the shadow. The most consideration is usually needed in

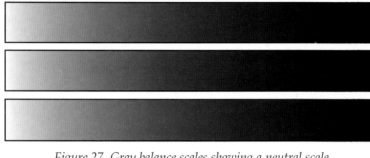

*Figure 27 Gray balance scales showing a neutral scale,
a scale with too much magenta and yellow (appears too warm) and
a scale without enough magenta and yellow (appears too cool)*

Removing the color cast requires that the operator determine which image areas to change. A tonal gradation change, by reducing or increasing one or two colors in the highlight, middletone or shadow areas, may be needed. A change in the tonal scale is an overall image change. Most color casts are overall, rather than in certain color areas. Whether you add color or remove color depends on whether the reproduction is too light or too dark.

Figure 28 Color cast removal

No unsharp masking

Unsharp masking 75, radius pixels 3, threshold 5

Unsharp masking 95, radius pixels 5, threshold 8

Figure 29 Unsharp masking examples

the middletone areas. The dot size values in the Figure 22 chart will produce grays for most printing conditions.

Color scanner color correction algorithms do not automatically correct in gray areas. Therefore, special attention must be paid to

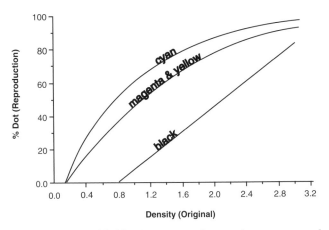

Figure 30 Typical halftoning curves that produce a gray scale for most printing conditions. This balance of curves is universal.

reducing the magenta and yellow dot sizes throughout the gray areas of the reproduction. When the original is viewed on the computer monitor and checked with the software's densitometer function, a neutral gray should always have a smaller magenta and yellow dot size than the cyan dot size. If the three are equal, a brown, rather than a neutral gray, will print. A neutral gray requires that you reduce the amount of magenta and yellow, or add cyan, in that area. Most desktop software programs allow you to fine-tune gray balance by simply adjusting the gradation, so that less magenta and yellow are printing.

Removing a color cast

A *color cast* is an overall unwanted color tinting of the original copy. It may be predominant in the highlight, shadow or middle-tone. However, it probably will occur in all of the picture content. It may have been caused by exposure, development or a film problem.

Removal of the unwanted cast will be accomplished by making changes to the contrast at it affects all color areas and neutrals. First, you must determine whether the cast is more pronounced in the highlight, middletone or shadows. Then, you ascertain which printer, cyan, magenta or yellow, needs to be reduced to remove the cast. For example, the highlight might have a pink cast. By reducing the printing dot size in the magenta highlight slightly, the color cast will be removed. Another way to remove the cast is by placing the values for gray in that patch. This will automatically remove the color cast. A white shirt is again white and not pink.

The color cast is removed from the separations by reducing the appropriate dot size in the needed separation areas. For serious casts, some operators only remove half of the cast to avoid a dramatic change. See Figure 28 for an example of color cast removal.

Using unsharp masking (USM)

Unsharp masking (USM) is an old photographic term, describing a method of compensating for a lack of sharpness in the original. The lack of sharpness may be inherent in the original or may be due to the color scanner optics. Using USM, the detail and apparent image sharpness is enhanced. Throughout the picture, the contrast is increased wherever there is an edge between two areas. That might be between a light and a dark, or between one color and another. The light edge is made even lighter than normal, or about one pixel wider, and the dark pixels are darkened. This is done in all four printers. It usually puts a little black line around one side of an edge and a light line along the other.

The secret to unsharp masking is adding the right amount to obtain detail, while not making the correction an unwanted attribute. The correct amount of unsharp masking is a matter of operator judgment, as well as a function of the size of the final reproduction. A larger reproduction may not need as much unsharp masking as a small reproduction. Sometimes when an image is enlarged, the unsharp masking is also enlarged. If you are aware of this, it will not be a problem.

On some drum scanners, unsharp masking is done by optical methods. During scanning, an extra photomultiplier detects when a change is coming. It adds that signal to the main color channels to get the edge blip on the image edges. On these scanners, aperture size and intensity settings adjustments can affect the strength and width of the unsharp edges.

When doing digital separations the software detects an edge by comparing the pixels stored in the picture file. In this case, you can adjust how many pixels wide the effect will be. In addition, you can indicate how much difference there must be before USM takes effect. To produce the best color reproduction detail, some USM is always necessary.

Handling a very grainy original

The graininess of an original can be exaggerated with unsharp masking (USM). Therefore, with grainy originals, it may be necessary to soften or reduce the USM amount. A drum scanner technique is to defocus the image so that the optics do not see the graininess. Therefore, the scanner cannot resolve the graininess. In Adobe Photoshop use the despeckle filter to remove the graininess.

Calibrating your color monitor

To achieve good color reproductions, the separation files are displayed on the color monitor and adjusted. Therefore, when the monitor is used, you must have confidence that the monitor display is accurate and calibrated.

Color monitors can be calibrated by visually comparing an image on the monitor with a color reproduction. The image in the separation files displayed and the reproduced image with which the files are being compared should be the same. For the most accurate visual comparison, a soft proof viewing booth is placed immediately next to the video monitor. *A **soft proof viewing booth** has 5000 degrees Kelvin (5000K) illumination. The light source has adjustable intensity that makes it possible to match the viewing box's light strength with that of the monitor. The printed reproduction is placed in the viewing booth, and the picture file of the same reproduction is shown on the monitor screen. This setup is used to evaluate and adjust the image on the monitor screen.

You should follow these color monitor calibration steps:

1. Obtain a printed reproduction of a picture file and the file.
2. Place the printed reproduction in the color viewing booth.
3. Place the viewing booth beside the monitor and adjust its light intensity to match the monitor's light intensity.
4. Compare the reproduction on the monitor screen with the printed sample in the viewing booth visually, side-by-side.
5. Set the color monitor's color temperature (the white point in degrees Kelvin) using the software profiles or preferences. It may be possible to use special color probes and software to accurately calibrate the video monitor color temperatures.
6. Adjust the color monitor's gamma correction for contrast, saturation and brightness so that the monitor image matches the printed reproduction. The **gamma correction** does what some

people misinterpret as color correction, because it changes the middletones and "cleans up" the picture.

7. Leave the settings unaltered between calibration sessions.

8. Tape over the monitor controls to avoid any accidental changes.

The effect of ambient lighting conditions on monitor accuracy

Lighting conditions must be considered when the monitor is being set up for color image evaluation. Ambient lighting, the existing light present on all sides of the monitor display, greatly influences the image's visual appearance. The surrounding light near the monitor should be about a five foot-candle illumination. This is very dark. No light sources in the area should shine directly on the monitor screen. Rather, soft indirect light should shine on the ceiling in that area.

Color management systems (CMS)

If you are working with a desktop color system, you need to have confidence that all the system parts are calibrated and accurate. You want certainty that what you see at each stage of production looks exactly like the final reproduction—commonly referred to as "What You See Is What You Get" (WYSIWYG).

Color management systems (CMS) are software algorithms. They make it possible to characterize each peripheral device and readjust its color space using gamut mapping. This insures that an image from each peripheral device matches the final output for color and brightness. Input scanners, video monitors and digital color proofers can be gamut mapped for specific printing conditions. Eventually CMSs will be included with all peripheral devices.

MAKING DESKTOP SEPARATIONS

Step-by-step desktop separations

Making good separations depends on your ability to configure your scanner and separation software to compensate for the printing conditions, the original's characteristics and the desires of the customer. The separation process requires that you take the steps listed below:

1. Set the scanner or software default conditions for the dot gain, GCR (gray component replacement),[6] total percent printing dot,[7] dot gain, and the dot sizes necessary for your printing conditions.
2. Set your color monitor preferences for 5000K neutral gray balance and proper gamma (contrast).
3. Set the scanner parameters for resolution and file size. This can be maximized by adjusting for the final size, the original type, pixels scanned per inch and halftone lines per inch. Another way to maximize the resolution and minimize the file size is to make the color scan of only the needed image area. Sometimes there is considerable picture area outside the area

---

[6] *GCR (gray component replacement)* is a scanning algorithm that can reproduce the gray component or darkening effect without changing the color's hue in a reproduction. The cyan, magenta and yellow dot sizes are reduced, and the black dot sizes in any given area are increased. GCR is used because it increases detail in the shadows, produces more consistent color and possibly saves ink. It reduces the total percent dot area printing.

[7] *Total percent printing dot* is the total amount of printing dot in a given area on a press sheet or on the separation films.

to be reproduced. There is no need to clutter the file storage with this unneeded information. This is especially important if you are using an automatic highlight-shadow adjustment algorithm. If you scan outside the needed image area, the algorithm may try to adjust to the wrong data.

4. Make the scan of the original.
5. Resize the image to the final reproduction size.
6. Adjust the scanned image for the correct highlight dot size and shadow dot size.
7. Adjust the middletone contrast to achieve the correct brightness and cleanliness, based on the monitor image and the keyness[8] of the copy.
8. Check and adjust the gray balance, if necessary.
9. Adjust the gradation[9] controls to remove any color cast.
10. Apply unsharp masking to enhance the picture detail.
11. Convert the file, if necessary, from an RGB mode to a CMYK mode for printing.
12. If the image looks correct, save the files in a file format that is best for your system or service bureau. EPS (encapsulated PostScript)[10] is one format that works very well. You may want to also save the files in DCS (desktop color separation) format. It is used for dropping images into a page makeup program, such as QuarkXPress or Aldus PageMaker. The DCS format stores preseparated four-color files and a place holder file. This speeds up color proofing and output to film, because

---

[8]*Keyness* see footnote 4, page 43.

[9]*Gradation* is the visual tonal relationship, the difference between light and dark areas, or the difference between highlights, middletones and shadow areas between an original image and its reproduction.

[10]*EPS (encapsulated PostScript)* is a graphic file format developed by Adobe Systems. EPS is used for PostScript graphic files that are to be incorporated into larger PostScript documents. The Mac version and the PC version differ in the viewfile. On the PC, it is in TIFF format or Microsoft Windows metafile format, and on the Mac, it is in PICT format.

the separations are already made and do not have to be remade during output. Some operators prefer TIFF format with the DCS separations and find it faster and a more accurate fit to the picture boxes.

Color separation software packages for the desktop

Color scanners capture the image as digital picture information and download it to the computer RAM memory for additional processing using color separation software. Image capturing programs either capture the image with the modifications for the printing characteristics and the original, or they offer the ability to modify the scanned image after scanning. Most separation software does not offer special image retouching functions.

There are many color separation programs available for the desktop computer. Some programs emulate highend scanner functions and require a degree of skill. Others are designed for beginners and can be used to make image modifications without much previous experience. Some computer programs are easier to use than others. Some give better color images than others. The following list contains some of the currently available programs.

EFI's Cachet is probably the most easy to use color separation program. It allows you to capture the image and visually modify both contrast and color balance. Without a great deal of experience, a person can adjust the contrast and achieve good separations from any original. The captured image is displayed on the video monitor in the center of a ring of the same image. Each image in the ring contains a different contrast. By clicking on the ring-around image that you like best, you automatically get a corrected image with the new contrast. A new ring-around image forms to give you another comparison to see if you want to change the reproduction further, or go back to the way it was.

In Cachet, the color balance in the captured image can also be changed by displaying the original image with all the possible ring-around changes for color balance. Once a corrected image is selected, that becomes the central image with a new ring-around of color cast variations. The image can be changed further, or it can be returned to its former image.

Adobe Photoshop is a program that captures images from many scanners and can be used for image manipulations and retouching, similar to a CEPS. For someone who wants to do everything on the desktop with one program, this is a very powerful one. It has the capacity for storing your printing parameters, as well as your monitor calibration parameters. Your printing condition limits are loaded, and the scan is captured. The image information is adjusted for highlight, shadow and middletones, similar to the way other software packages do. Some of the image retouching functions available in the program are cloning,[11] resizing,[12] special effects filters, airbrushing,[13] spot removal,[14] etc. . . .

Aldus Preprint is designed to capture images and facilitate adjustments for tone reproduction and saturation. This is not an image retouching program.

Human Software Company's ColorExtreme can acquire, separate and enhance RGB and Kodak Photo CD images on the fly and offers

---

[11] *Cloning,* or *pixel swopping,* is an image processing function that is used to duplicate a pixel or many pixels from one picture area to another picture area. This function can be used to add or remove detail.

[12] *Resizing* is an image processing function that changes the size of the image.

[13] *Airbrushing* is an image processing function that adds or removes printing ink content in a designated picture area. A stylus on a digitizing tablet can be adjusted for spray strength, speed and width to initiate the changes.

[14] *Spot removal* is an image processing function that removes unwanted "hickeys."

batch processing of up to 100 photos. It can also do retouching and can create Adobe Illustrator-compatible vector paths to export and output design and retouching functions.

Light Source's Ofoto makes separations and adjusts for printing parameters. It has an autoscan mode that automatically determines highlight and shadow points. This function can be turned off for manual adjustments. Ofoto is not a color manipulation or retouching program.

Monaco System's Binuscan performs a scan and carries out a histogram analysis to establish the correct tone compression and color balance. It automatically sets highlight and shadow points and applies unsharp masking to the scan.

Pixel Craft's ColorAccess and *Pre-Press Technologies' Spectre-Print Pro* emulate the functionality of a highend scanner. Many operators have said that they like the quality obtainable with these programs. Although these programs manipulate images much like a highend scanner, they are not color retouching applications. They do not emulate a CEPS.

Optronic's ColorRight 4.0 is a Mac-based program that performs RGB-CMYK conversions and USM on the fly.

There are several color retouching programs available. However, it is not the purpose of this book to study retouching programs.

Imagesetter calibration

An imagesetter is a peripheral device designed to expose images on film. The imagesetter converts digitally stored page or separation information from file format to film format. The film contains the text, graphics, black and white halftones and color separations. The imagesetter has become the output device for desktop page makeup and color separations, as desktop scanners do not have their own film plotters. To provide the films for the later platemaking step, the desktop page or color separation file either has to go back to a high-end scanner, a CEPS or an imagesetter for output exposure.

Because of the degree of accuracy needed for good color separations, it is imperative that the operator calibrates the imagesetter precisely. To assure good results, every dot size from 0 to 100% in the file should reproduce on the film from 0 to 100%, respectively, within ±1% accuracy. Color Calibration Software is available to make the calibration in the RIP[15] to give accurate dot sizes on the film.

Imagesetters available today are capable of producing films without undesirable attributes or artifacts, such as moiré, image size problems, banding or fit difficulties. Halftone dots should change in size from 0% to 100% with a smooth gradation. *Banding* occurs when the gradation is interrupted by strips of greater or less than, desired dot sizes, caused by irregular film motion within the imagesetter. The stripes of irregular density run perpendicular to the direction of travel. *Fit* refers to maintaining the exact distances between images on the films. Fit and register are not synonyms.

Color proofing assures good color separation quality

A soft proof is a color separation digital file viewed on a computer video monitor to evaluate the image. It is a bit risky to certify the exact accuracy of a color separation set based on the video monitor image. Even though the video monitor has been calibrated, it may not have the same color gamut as the printing method. It is also a different geometry than the ink on paper will be. For this reason, it

---

[15] *RIP* is the abbreviation for raster image processor, a software program or computer that determines what value each pixel of a final output page bitmap should have based on commands from the page description language.

is accepted practice to make a color proof on a white substrate with pigments or dyes that simulate the process ink printing on paper. When the color proof is made from the halftone films, it is called an *analog proof*. It may be an *overlay proof* or *single sheet proof*. With the overlay proof, each layer of process color is on a separate carrier sheet and is overlaid on a piece of white paper. A single sheet proof transfers each process color to the white carrier sheet to simulate the printing as closely as possible. Both analog type proofs require that the films be output first in order to use them to make the proofs.

Digital files can be proofed without films using *direct digital color proofs (DDCP)*. These proofs are made on a printer that can accept the digitized image information directly from the computer. A cyan, magenta, yellow and black proof are created. The DDCP is not necessarily an exact replica of the halftone separations that will be made later on the imagesetter. However, if everything is calibrated properly, the DDCP will represent the hues, detail and contrast of the image that the film will produce.

There are many levels of color proofers, ranging in price from $1,000 to $150,000. Currently, the majority of these proofs are being used as pre-proofs. The direct digital color proof will become more popular as it becomes a more accurate simulation of the printed result. It is beginning to replace the analog proof as a *contract proof*. A contract proof represents an agreement between the printer and the customer regarding the expected, exact appearance of the printed product. Deviation from the proof is grounds for non-payment by the customer.

For any color proof to be useful, it must be accurate. It must be a true representation of the printing process. Therefore, before you can have faith in the proof's accuracy, you must make sure that the color proofing system is calibrated to match the printed result. That requires working backwards. The color proofing system is calibrated to visually match a previously printed reproduction or press sheet. Once calibration has been achieved, you can confidently proof color separations and know they will print like the proof. But this also requires that you have calibrated the system for consistency.

It should be pointed out that both the color proof and the printing process do not have to be made using the same color sequence. It is possible to use a color sequence in the proofing that visually simulates the color printing, but is not the same as the printing sequence. Often, the color proof has the black or cyan as the top color layer.

Viewing color proofs must be done under standard 5000K lighting conditions. Some proofing materials are *metameric*, which means that they appear differently under different lighting conditions. For accuracy, the color proof and the original, or the press sheet, should be viewed side-by-side under standard illumination. Fold the press sheet and lay it on the original, so that the same areas are in contact with one another. Your eyes are very good at making side-by-side color comparisons of color images. However, you do not have a good color memory. You cannot hold the proof in one hand and the press sheet in the other, and expect to remember the color as you look back and forth from one to the other. You must insist on a side-by-side comparison.

Standard viewing conditions

Standard color viewing conditions have been established worldwide. The following is a description of that standard:

1. The color of the light source must be equal to a black body heated to 5000 degrees Kelvin. There usually is an indication on the color viewing booth that it has a 5000K color temperature.
2. There should be a neutral gray surround on three sides of the viewing area to keep out light from other sources.

3. The color rendering index should be 90 to 100%. That means that all wavelengths of light are represented. This is a difficult measurement to make. You have to assume that the manufacturer of the color viewing booth has done its homework and that the booth is accurately made.

4. The bulb must be changed on a regular basis. It is recommended that after every 2500 hours of use, new bulbs be installed.

5. When the bulbs are first turned on, always allow a 15 minute warm-up period. This is necessary because during the startup time the bulbs give off a pink light. This light is not 5000K.

6. Put the transparency viewer inside the color viewing booth, so that the overhead light is on when looking at the transparency. This helps to insure that the transparency and color proof are viewed in a similar manner. Do not look at the transparency under darkened room conditions and at color proofs under lighted conditions. This will very quickly lead you astray. Under these conditions the original and the proof will not match.

Controlling the color printing

Controlling the printing is just as important as controlling the color separations. If you must be at the printing press certifying that the printing is being done correctly, your number one concern is: Does the color printing match the OK color proof for color hues, overall color balance and contrast? Your second concern is that accurate image register is maintained. Third, there should be no unwanted objectionable attributes such as hickeys, scratches, smudges, slurring,[16] doubling,[17] or ghosting.[18]

Throughout the pressrun the color *OK proof* or the color *OK press sheet*[19] should be kept handy for side-by-side comparison with each new press sheet being checked. Once a color OK press sheet is achieved, it is probably a better color reference than the OK proof. To maintain the match of the OK press sheet and the new color sheets off the press, it is important to maintain the hue accuracy. This should be done, even if it is necessary to adjust the ink levels separately. Maintaining the color balance of the overprint colors will also help to produce consistent hues. The *overprint colors* are blues, greens and reds. A change in their color strength is not as serious as a shift in their hue, for example, from red to orange. Most customers say that consistent hue throughout the pressrun is the most important criteria for good color reproduction. This also requires that color balance be maintained.

Only view the press sheets under standard 5000K illumination. Looking at them under any other non-standard illumination can greatly modify how the colors appear. It could possibly influence you to make a wrong decision about inking.

It is important to certify that all colors are kept in register within an accuracy of one row of dots. *Register* means that the images line up exactly, and that one color does not hang outside of another. Register within one row of dots is generally considered acceptable. Variation of two rows of dots is noticeable. Variation of three rows of dots is objectionable and probably not acceptable.

---

[16] *Slurring* is the smearing of the halftone dots on the press sheet in the direction of press sheet travel through the press. The halftone dots look like comets and result in dot gain.

[17] *Doubling* is a printing defect caused by a mechanical problem with the press. It causes a second set of dots to print between the desired set of dots on a press sheet halftone image. The unaided human eye sees this dot gain as a darkening of the color or a color shift.

[18] *Ghosting* is a weak image that appears in a heavy solid ink area of the image just ahead of the solid area that has taken away some of the ink from the rollers during the printing.

[19] *OK press sheet* is a press sheet taken from the press during the makeready or from the beginning of the pressrun, evaluated by the customer, marked "OK," signed and used as a color quality control guide during the rest of the pressrun. Also called pass sheet or color OK.

Double click on shadow eyedropper
Set C=95, M=82, Y=82, K=80, click **OK**
Double click on middletone eyedropper
Set C=62, M=50, Y=50, K=80, click **OK**

Drag Windows to Show Information (This opens Show Info pallet
  and brings up the densitometer.)
Turn ON densitometer to make dot area measurements

Make each separation for the original and the customer's d

When modifying your separation for the original's charac
and desired appearance:

*Make most color adjustments in RGB color spa
before changing the mode to CMYK*

1. Drag File to Acquire to scan in an image or oper

2. Drag Image to Image Size and input paramet
   Enter size desired for either horizontal or ve
     dimension is automatic.)
   Leave proportions ON. Click File size OF
   Click on auto
   Set screen ruling to desired value: Exar
     sheetfed coated; 133 line for webfec
     for webfed coated commercial; 10
   Click on quality required ("Best" a
     dot), click **OK**
   Resolution displays, pixels per i

   light, shadow and mi
         Adjust—Cur
         eyedrop
         ssary to
         eyedro
   K

2.5 was pre-

Making color separations for other printing processes

While this text has taught you how to make color separations for offset lithography, the techniques described will apply for all other printing processes. What changes are the preferences, defaults and the required dot sizes for the ink hues and the dot gains. If you can make good separations for offset lithography, you can make them for other processes. You must pay close attention to the dot gain of the process and compensate for it.

STEP-BY-STEP SEPARATIONS USING ADOBE PHOTOSHOP 2.5

Using Adobe Photoshop, four steps are required to make color separations.

1. Set up the preferences for your printing press
2. Capture and process the image.
3. Save the file.
4. Import the image into a page.

Set up Adobe Photoshop preferences for your printing press

The printing parameters are set to give good color reproductions when preparing files for printing on a printing press or calibrated direct digital color proofer. Each time you call in an image these preferences are ready for use. They remain in your file prefer-ences until you change them.

Open Photoshop and open an image
Drag File to Preferences—General
CMYK Composites: Click Faster
Click Channels in Color, click **OK**
Drag File to Preferences—Scratch Disks
Select startup or other, click **OK**

Drag File to Preferences—Monitor Setup
Gamma: 1.60
White point: 5000K
Phosphor colors: Name your monitor type
Ambient light: Medium, click **OK**

Drag Apple to Control Panel
Click on Gamma
Adjust Gamma to tone balance gray strip
Balance the white point, black point and middletones
the monitor gray scale. Compare to a photograph
Close file

Drag File to Preferences—Printing Inks Setup
Dot gain: Set to appropriate amount. Example:
coated; 22% webfed coated; 20% sheetfed u
webfed newsprint
Click **OK**

Drag File to Preferences—Separation Set
Separation type: Click GCR
Black generation: Medium
Black limit: 100%
Total ink limit: 300-320%
UCA[20] amount: 0%, click **OK**

Drag image to Adjust—Curves
Click on center of gray scale ur
side of graph
Double click on highlight eye
Set C=5, M=3, Y=3, K=0, cl

[20] *UCA (undercolor addition*
in the dark neutral areas. Th
dot sizes are reduced too n
may be lighter than desir
technique of reducing the thic
and compensating by increasing th
reproduced with fewer trapping problem.

COLOR SEPARATION ON THE DESKTOP

Click on center of curve and pull towards lower right to lighten
image. Stop movement to allow monitor to refresh the new
image. When you like the image contrast and detail, click **OK**

4. If picture contrast is too flat, drag Image to Adjust—
Brightness/Contrast, click **OK**
Increase contrast +10%, click **OK** to compute change. Or, use
Curves to redue highlight, increase shadow and adjust mid-
dletone curve

5. Sharpen image by dragging filters to Sharpen—Unsharp
Masking
Amount: depends on scanner type, original and resolution, try
a 75 to 200 range
Set Radius 1, Threshold 2, click **OK**

6. Change hues of basic CMY or RGB colors if needed
Drag image to Adjust—Hue/Saturation
Modify hue to desired color, click **OK**

7. Drag Mode from RGB to CMYK, click **OK**

8. Drag File to Save as:
Name of file:
File Format: Drag type to EPS and release
EPS box will ask "Desktop Color Separation" (5 files), these are
the DCS files.
Click Master file, 72 pixels/inch CMYK color
Indicate where to save files with desktop box and/or file name
box.
Click **OK**

9. This image is now ready for importing into a picture box
QuarkXPress or Aldus PageMaker.[21]

[21] The procedure for step-by-step separations using
pared with information furnished by Jim Rich

COLOR REFERENCES*

Books, videos and disks

The format for listing the color references is: title, author, year published, number of pages, binding type, publisher, price and retail outlet. See Sources of literature for explanations of abbreviations.

4 Colors and One Image
  Matthias Nyman
  1993, 96 pages, softcover, Peachpit, $18, Peachpit

47 Printing Headaches (and How to Avoid Them)
  Linda Sanders
  1991, 144 pages, softcover, North Light, $24.95, North Light

1001 Hints & Tips for the Macintosh
  Erica Litsky and Tracy Hines
  1991, 170 pages, softcover, Ziff-Davis, free, MacUser

Adobe Illustrator, 3.0, (3rd edition)
  Tony Bove, Fred Davis and Cheryl Rhodes
  1991, 448 pages, softcover, Bantam, $26.95, GAP

Adobe Illustrator, 5.0
  Tony Bove and Cheryl Rhodes
  1993, 432 pages, softcover, Bantam, $26.95, GAP

Adobe Illustrator for Windows: Classroom in a Book
  Adobe Systems
  1993, 320 pages, softcover, Hayden, $44.95, GAP

Adobe Photoshop for Windows: Classroom in a Book
  Adobe Systems
  1993, 320 pages, softcover, Hayden, $44.95, GAP

Adobe Photoshop Handbook, The Official, 2nd edition
  David Biedny and Bert Monroy
  1993, 480 pages, softcover, Bantam, $28.95, GAP & Color Res

* Prices listed are non-member prices. Members of some organizations receive price discounts that are not listed here. Some distributors also offer multiple copy discounts. Contact Graphic Arts Publishing for a more complete listing of color reproduction books.

Adobe Photoshop/Mac: Classroom in a Book
Adobe Systems
1993, 320 pages, softcover, Prentice-Hall, $44.95

Adobe Photoshop Version 2.5 in Black and White
Jim Rich and Sandy Bozek
1993, 43 pages, softcover, Bozek, $19.95, Bozek and Rich

American National Standard for Graphic Arts and Photography—Color Prints, Transparencies, and Photomechanical Reproductions–Viewing Conditions
Charles Saleski
1989, 9 pages, softcover, ANSI, free with purchase of *ANSI Ph2.30-1989 For Graphic Arts and Photographic Color Prints, Transparencies and Photomechanical Viewing Conditions*, GCA

ANPA-Color: Ad-Litho/AdPro Color Ink Book
Anonymous
1987, 60 pages, hardcover, ANPA, $50, ANPA

Applied Densitometry
William Sullivan, compiler and Paul Borkowski, editor
1991, 18 pages, softcover, Gretag, free, Automation Eng

Basic Law of Color Theory, The
Harald Kueppers
1980, 220 pages, softcover, Barrons, $7.95, RIT Bkst, Barrons, & Tools

Best of the Desktop Publishing Forum on CompuServe, The
Thom Hartmann
1993, 260 pages, softcover, Peachpit, $25, Peachpit

Beyond the Desktop: Tools and Technology for Computer Publishing
Barry Sosinsky
1991, 732 pages, softcover, Bantam, $29.95, GAP

Bridges
Anonymous
1991, floppy disk, Prepress Tech, $39.95, Hoechst Celanese

Camera Ready with QuarkXPress
Cyndie Klopfenstein
1993, 224 pages with Mac template disk, Peachpit, $35, Peachpit

CEPS Video Program
Anonymous
1990, 105 min., video, IPA, $200, IPA

Color: A Guide to Basic Facts and Concepts
R.W. Burnham, R.M. Hanes and C.J. Bartleson
1963, 250 pages, hardcover, John Wiley, out of print

Color and Human Response
  Faber Birren
  1978, 120 pages, softcover, Van Nostrand, $16.95, Tools

Color and Its Reproduction
  Gary G. Field
  1988, 392 pages, softcover, GATF, $65, GATF & GAP

Color Atlas: A Practical Guide for Color Mixing
  Harald Kueppers
  1982, 176 pages, softcover, Barrons, $10.95, Barrons & RIT Bkst

Color Bars, An Introduction to
  Peter Brehm
  1992, 66 pages, softcover, GCA, $39.95, GCA

Color Compendium, The
  Augustine Hope and Margaret Walch
  1990, 360 pages, hardcover, Van Nostrand, $49.95, Van Nostrand

Color Desktop Publishing Product Annual
  Maury Zeff and Thad McIlroy
  1992, 250 pages, ring binder, Color Res, $95, Color Res

Color Expert 1.0: the interface of design and printing
  Color Expert
  1993, CD tutorial plus 64 page booklet, Color Expert, $395

Color for the Electronic Age
  Jan V. White
  1990, 208 pages, softcover, Watson-Guptill, $32.50, Watson-Guptill

Color Harmony: A Guide to Creative Color Combinations
  Hideaki Chijiiwa
  1987, 152 pages, softcover, North Light, $15.95, RIT Bkst & North Light

Color in Business, Science and Industry
  Deane B. Judd
  1961, 402 pages, hardcover, John Wiley, $79.95, John Wiley & RIT Bkst

Color in the 21st Century
  Helene Eckstein
  1991, 160 pages, softcover, Watson-Guptill, $29.95, Watson-Guptill

Color Mac, The
  Marc Miller and Randy Zaucha
  1992, 334 pages, softcover, Hayden, $39.95, GAP, Color Res

Color on Color
  Richard Emery
  1993, 160 pages, softcover, North Light, $34.95, GAP

Color Publishing on the Mac
   Kim and Sunny Baker
   1992, 479 pages, softcover, Random House, $45, GAP & Color Res

Color Publishing on the PC
   Kim and Sunny Baker
   1993, 526 pages, softcover, Random House, $45, GAP & Color Res

Color References: Hi-Lo and Single Level
   Anonymous
   yearly, 1 page, printed color swatches, IPA, $52, IPA

Color Scanners: A Comparison Chart
   Durbin Associates
   1991, 14 pages + 6 charts, softcover, Durbin, $25, Durbin

Color Scanning and Imaging Systems
   Gary G. Field
   1990, 315 pages, softcover, GATF, $65, GATF & GAP

Color Separation on the Desktop
   Miles Southworth and Donna Southworth
   1993, 96 pages, softcover, GAP, $16.95, GAP & Color Res

Color-Separation Scanner, The (Q-78)
   James Radenbaugh, editor
   1981, 24 pages, softcover, EKCo, $7.50, EKCo

Color Separation Techniques, 3rd edition
   Miles Southworth
   1989, 264 pages, softcover, GAP, out of print

Color Source Book I
   Anonymous
   1989, 112 pages, softcover, North Light, $15.95, North Light

Color Spaces and PostScript Level 2
   Jim Hamilton
   1991, 4 pages, one bulletin in the *Linotype-Hell Technical Information Notebook*,
   Linotype-Hell, one free, Linotype-Hell/Hamilton

Color Stripping: A Guide for Process Color Image Assembly
   Malcolm Keif
   1992, 61 pages, softcover, Graphic Ser Pub, $12.50, GAP

Colorworks: The Designer's Ultimate Guide to Working with Color, (5 books)
   Dale Russell
   1990, 144 pages per book, softcover, North Light, $24.95 each, North Light

Colour Reproduction in the Printing Industry
   Anthony Mortimer
   1992, 233 pages, softcover, Pira, £40, Pira

Colour Theory and Scanning for Prepress
David Whelan
1992, 80 pages, softcover, David Whelan, $17, Winchcombe

Complete Color Glossary, The Color Resource
Miles Southworth, Thad McIlroy and Donna Southworth
1992, 240 pages, hardcover, Color Res/GAP, $24.95, GAP, Color Res, RIT Bkst, RIT T&E, NAPL, & PIA

Complete Guide to Trapping
Brian Lawler
1993, 87 pages, softcover, Color Res, $24.95, GAP & Color Res

Complete MacPrePress, Vol. I, The
Steve Hannaford and Kathleen Tinkel
1991, 210 pages, softcover, Color Res, $99, Color Res

Complete MacPrePress, Vol. II, The
Steve Hannaford and Kathleen Tinkel
1992, 210 pages, softcover, Color Res, $99, Color Res

Complete Scanner Handbook for Desktop Publishing: Macintosh Edition, The
David D. Busch
1991, 386 pages, softcover, Business One Irwin, $24.95, Business One Irwin

Computer Color: 10,000 Computer-Generated Process Colors
Michael and Pat Rogondino
1990, 108 pages, spiral, Chronicle, $24.95, Chronicle

Computer Color Matching for Gravure Printing
Anonymous
1987, 27 pages, softcover, GAA, $30, GAA

Controlling Color: A Practical Introduction for Designers and Artists
Patricia Lambert
1991, 92 pages, softcover, McGraw-Hill, $16.95, Color Res

Corel/DRAW: Visual QuickStart Guide, 4th edition
Webster & Associates
1993, 400 pages, softcover, Peachpit, $16, Peachpit

Cost Study on Desktop/Electronic Publishing Operations
Donald Goldman and Charles Alessandrina
1993, approx. 59 pages, softcover, NAPL, $100, NAPL

Data Transmission for the Graphic Arts Industry
Melene Follert
1987, 80 pages, softcover, NCA, $19.95, Follert

Dead Mac Scrolls
Larry Pina
1992, 484 pages, softcover, Peachpit, $32, Peachpit

Densitometry Made in Switzerland
Anonymous
1991, 30 pages, softcover, Gretag, free, Automation Eng

Designer Photoshop
Rob Day
1993, 250 pages, softcover, Random House, $30, GAP

Designer's Guide to Color Combinations
James Stockton
1984, 124 pages, softcover, Chronicle, $9.95, Tools

Design Essentials
Luanne Cohen, Russell Brown, Lisa Jeans and Tanya Wendling
1992, 102 pages, softcover, Hayden, $39.95, GAP

Designing with Color
Roy Osborne
1991, 144 pages, hardcover, North Light, $26.95, North Light

DE$KTOP DIVIDEND$: Managing Electronic Prepress for Profit
Philip Ruggles
1993, 188 pages, softcover, Prtg Mgmt Serv, $23.95, GAP

Desktop Publisher's Idea Book, The
Chuck Green
1993, 336 pages, softcover, Bantam, $21.95, GAP

Desktop Publisher's Survival Kit
David Blatner
1991, 184 pages, softcover, Peachpit, $22.95, Peachpit

Desktop Publishing in Black + White & Color
Thad McIlroy and Gord Graham
1992, 180 pages, softcover, Color Res, $49, GAP & Color Res

Desktop Publishing in Color
Michael Kieran
1991, 384 pages, softcover, Bantam, $26.95, GAP & Color Res

Desktop Publishing Opportunities for the Commercial Printer
M.L Blum and M.B. McKean
1990, 289 pages, 3 ring notebook, GATF, $195, GATF

Desktop Publishing Success: How to Start and Run a Desktop Publishing Business
Felix Kramer and Maggie Lovaas
1991, 350 pages, softcover, Business One Irwin, $29.95, Business One Irwin

Desktop Typography with QuarkXPress
Frank Romano
1988, 209 pages, softcover, GAMA, $19.95, GAMA & Tools

Digital Color Prepress, An Introduction to
Steven Hannaford
1990, 32 pages, softcover, Agfa, $10, Agfa

Digital Color Prepress, Vol II
Steve Hannaford
1991, 32 pages, softcover, Agfa, $10, Agfa

Digital Exchange Standards for the GA
Tom Dunn
1990, Dunn Tech, $2500, Dunn Tech

Digital Proofing Defined
D. Greifenkamp, G. Frazier, N. Lombardi and M. Winn
1991, 6 pages, softcover, GCA, free, GCA

Double-Dot/Duotone Guide
Harvey Sternbach
1991, 226 pages, hardcover, NAPL, $79.50, NAPL

Electronic Color Separation
R. K. Molla
1988, 288 pages, hardcover, R.K. Prtg Pub, $61.95, R.K. Prtg Pub, PIA, NAPL, RIT Bkst, & Tools

Electronic Color: The Art of Color Applied to Graphic Computing
Richard B. Norman
1991, 186 pages, softcover, Van Nostrand, $59.95, Tools

Electronic Design and Publishing: Business Practices
Liane Sebastian
1992, 130 pages, softcover, Allworth Press, $19.95, GAP

Electronic Imaging Applications in Graphic Arts: Proceedings
Kennard Cloud, editor
1989, 142 pages, softcover, SPIE, $44, SPIE

Electronic Type Catalog, The
Steve Byers
1992, 640 pages, softcover, Bantam, $34.95, GAP

Elements of Color
Johannes Itten
1982, 96 pages, softcover, Van Nostrand, $19.95, Tools & RIT Bkst

EMS: Electronic Mechanical Specifications
GCA Electronic Front End Study Group
1992, 17 pages, softcover, GCA, $11.75, GAP & Color Res

Encapsulated PostScript: Application Guide for the Macintosh and PC
Peter Vollenweider
1990, 220 pages, softcover, Prentice-Hall Int'l Ltd (UK), $34.67, Prentice-Hall

Evaluating High Performance Color Scanners
Jim Rich
1993, 48 pages, softcover, Rich, $95, GAP & Color Res

Evolution in Color
Frans Gerritsen, from Dutch by Edward Force
1988, 88 pages, softcover, Schiffer, $14.95, Schiffer

Fit to Print with QuarkXPress
Lauren Smith
1992, 335 pages, softcover, M&T, $32.95, Color Res

Flexography: Principles and Practices, 4th edition
Frank Siconolfi, editor
1991, 549 pages, softcover, FFTA, $95, FFTA

Focoltone Color Charts
Gordon Phillips
1990, notebook, fanbook, Focoltone

GCA/GATF Proof Comparator II
Anonymous
1986, films, GCA or GATF, $84, GCA & GATF

GCA GCR Application Guide
Anonymous
1992, 1 page, poster, GCA, $13, GCA

GCA Measure 21 Process Guide
Anonymous
1988, 12 pages, 8-1/2 x 11 & 11/17 foldout chart, GCA, $7.50, GCA

GCA "T-Ref"
Anonymous
yearly, 1 page, GCA, $85, GCA

Getting It Printed, 2nd edition
Mark Beach
1993, 208 pages, softcover, Coast to Coast, $29.95, Coast to Coast, GAP

Giving a Color OK: How to Prepare and What to Do
Robert Jose
1990, 4 pages, notebook, GAP, $8, GAP & GCA

Glossary: The World of Prepress Terminology
SGAUA Committee
1991, 6 floppy disks, SGAUA, $49.95, SGAUA

Graphic Arts Photography: Color
Fred Wentzel, Ray Blair and Tom Destree
1987, 160 pages, softcover, GATF, $45, GATF & GAP

Graphic Designer's Production Handbook
Norman Sanders and William Bevington
1982, 195 pages, softcover, Hastings, $10.95, Hastings

Gravure Process and Technology
Brett Rutherford, editor
1991, 500 pages, hardcover, GEF & GAA, $70, GAA

Gravure Publication Ink Manual
Anonymous
1983, 138 pages, softcover, GAA, $45, GAA

Great Design Using 1, 2 & 3 Colors
Supon Design Group
1993, 192 pages, softcover, North Light, $39.95, North Light

Guide for choosing the correct viewing conditions for colour publishing
Tony Johnson and Marcus Scott-Taggart
1993, softcover, Pira, £35, Pira

Guide to Graphic Arts Densitometry
Anonymous
1992, 8 pages, X-Rite, free, X-Rite

Guide to Quality Reproduction: USA Today, A
Anonymous
1987, 24 pages, softcover, USA Today, free, USA Today

Guide to Understanding Color Communication
Anonymous
1990, 18 pages, X-Rite, free, X-Rite

Hard Copy and Printing Technologies: Proceedings
Ken-Ichi Shimazu, editor
1990, 252 pages, softcover, SPIE, $55, SPIE

Hard Copy Output: Proceedings
Leo Beiser, editor
1989, 500 pages, softcover, SPIE, $84, SPIE

How to Check and Correct Color Proofs
David Bann and John Gargan
1990, 144 pages, hardcover, North Light, $27.95, GAP, Color Res & others

How to Make Great Gray-Scale Images
Anonymous
1991, softcover, Image-In, free, Image-In

How to make sure what you see is what you get!
Peter Fink
1993, 28 pages, softcover, Merritt, $6.99, GAP & Merritt

How to Understand and Use Design & Layout
  Alan Swann
  1991, 144 pages, softcover, North Light, $19.95, North Light

IBM PC and PS/2 Graphics Handbook
  Ed Teja and Laura Johns
  1990, 419 pages, softcover, Microtrend, $24.95, Microtrend

Illustrator Illuminated
  Clay Andres
  1992, 161 pages, softcover, Peachpit, $24.95, Color Res

Inside Adobe Illustrator 4.0 for Windows
  New Riders Publishing
  1993, 800 pages, softcover, Prentice-Hall, $34.95

Inside Adobe Photoshop: The Digital Darkroom
  Gary Bouton
  1993, 700 pages, softcover, Prentice-Hall, $34.95, GAP

Inside Photo CD: Market Opportunities in a Leading Edge Technology
  Thad McIlroy and David Pease, editors
  1993, 150 pages, softcover, Color Res, $195, Color Res

Interactions of Color
  Josef Albers
  1975, 81 pages, softcover, Yale, $6.95, Yale

Introduction to Color Bars
  Peter Brehm
  1992, 64 pages, softcover, GCA, $39.95, GCA & GAP

Introduction to Densitometry
  Peter Brehm
  1990, 62 pages, softcover, GCA, $28.50, GCA & GAP

Introduction to Digital Color Prepress
  Steve Hannaford
  1992, 29 slide presentation plus booklet, $125, Color Res

LIG/EDP '90 Conference Proceedings Vol. I&II
  Patrice Dunn and Henry Lassiter, editors
  1991, 326 & 366 pages, softcover, Dunn Tech, $495 or $265/volume, Dunn Tech

LIG/EDP '91 Conference Proceedings
  Patrice Dunn, editor
  1992, 400 pages, softcover, Dunn Tech, $100, Dunn Tech

Linotronic Imaging Handbook: The Desktop Publishers Guide to High Quality Text and Images
  James Cavuoto and Stephen Beale
  1990, 217 pages, softcover, Micro Pub, $27.95, Micro Pub & GAMA

Linotype-Hell Screen Angle and Ruling Tester
  1990, film screen tester, Linotype-Hell, free, Linotype-Hell

Linotype-Hell Technical Information Notebook
  Jim Hamilton
  1991-3, collection of bulletins, notebook, Linotype-Hell, $99, Linotype-Hell

MAC-graphics: A Designer's Guide to Graphics for the Apple Macintosh
  Anonymous
  1990, 288 pages, spiral, Design Press, $49.95, Design Press

Macintosh Bible, The, 4th edition
  Arthur Naiman, Nancy Dunn, Susan McCallister, John Kadyk and others
  1993, 1241 pages, Peachpit, $32, Peachpit

Macintosh Bible "WHAT DO I DO NOW?" Book, The, 2th edition
  Charles Rubin
  1992, 352 pages, Peachpit, $15, Peachpit

Macintosh Digital Photography Primer
  George Wedding
  1993, 400 pages, softcover, Hayden, $49.95

Making Art on the Macintosh
  Michael Gosney and Linnea Dayton
  1989, 318 pages, softcover, Scott Foresman, $22.95, Scott Foresman

Mastering Adobe Illustrator
  David Holzgang
  1988, 330 pages, softcover, Sybex, $24.95, GAMA

Mastering CorelDraw 3
  Chris Dickman
  1993, 574 pages, softcover, Peachpit, $38, Color Res

Measuring Colour, 2nd edition
  R.W.G. Hunt
  1991, 313 pages, hardcover, Horwood, $74, Automation Eng

Mechanical Color Separation Skills for the Commercial Artist
  Tom Cardamone
  1980, 128 pages, softcover, Van Nostrand, $19.95, Van Nostrand & Tools

Munsell Nearly Neutral Color Book and Fan Deck
  Anonymous
  1991, fan deck, notebook, chart, Macbeth, $12-$675, Macbeth

Neugebauer Memorial Seminar on Color Reproduction: Proceedings,
  Kazuo Sayanagi, editor
  1989, 204 pages, softcover, SPIE, $64, SPIE

PageMaker 4: An Easy Desk Reference, Mac Edition
    Robin Williams
    1991, 784 pages, softcover, Peachpit, $29.95, Peachpit

PageMaker 4: An Easy Desk Reference, Windows Edition
    Robin Williams
    1991, 784 pages, softcover, Peachpit, $29.95, Peachpit

PageMaker 4: Visual Quick Start Guide, Mac Edition
    Webster & Associates
    1991, 200 pages, softcover, Peachpit, $12.95, Peachpit

PageMaker 5 Expert Techniques, Macintosh Edition
    Michael Nolan
    1993, 208 pages, softcover, Hayden, $34.95

PageMaker 5 Expert Techniques, Windows Edition
    Michael Nolan
    1993, 208 pages, softcover, Hayden, $34.95

PageMaker 5 Tips & Tricks, Mac Edition
    Stephen F. Roth and Olav Martin Kvern
    1993, 320 pages w/disk, Peachpit, $25, Peachpit

PageMaker 5 Tips & Tricks, Windows Edition
    Stephen F. Roth and Olav Martin Kvern
    1993, 320 pages w/disk, Peachpit, $25, Peachpit

PageMaker 5: Visual Quick Start Guide, Mac Edition
    Webster & Associates
    1993, 200 pages, softcover, Peachpit, $14, Peachpit

PageMaker 5: Visual Quick Start Guide, Windows Edition (2nd edition)
    Webster & Associates
    1993, 200 pages, softcover, Peachpit, $14, Peachpit

Perceiving, Measuring and Using Color, *Proceedings*
    Michael Brill, editor
    1990, 312 pages, softcover, SPIE, $55, SPIE

Photo CD: Quality Photos at Your Fingertips
    John Larish
    1993, 206 pages, softcover, Micro Pub, $27.95, GAP & Color Res

Photographing for Publications: A Guide for Photographers
    Norman Sanders
    1984, 112 pages, softcover, Bowker, $44.95, Tools

Photography for Reproduction
    Anonymous
    1990, 84 pages, softcover, S.D. Warren, free, S.D. Warren

Photoshop 2.5 for Macintosh: Visual QuickStart Guide
Elaine Weinmann and Peter Lourekas
1993, 270 pages, Peachpit, $18, Peachpit

Photoshop 2.5 for Windows: Visual QuickStart Guide
Elaine Weinmann and Peter Lourekas
1993, 270 pages, Peachpit, $18, Peachpit

Photoshop Handbook, The Official
David Biedny and Bert Monroy
1991, 423 pages, softcover, Bantam, $26.50, GAP

Photoshop Wow! Book, The, Macintosh 2.5 Edition
Linnea Dayton and Jack Davis
1993, 208 pages w/disk, Peachpit, $35, Peachpit

Photoshop Wow! Book, The, Windows 2.5 Edition
Linnea Dayton and Jack Davis
1993, 208 pages w/disk, Peachpit, $35, Peachpit

Picture Perfect Computer Output for Computer Graphics
Jan Rowell
1990, 72 pages, softcover, Tektronix, $15, Tektronix

Pocket Guide to Color Reproduction, 3rd edition
Miles Southworth and Donna Southworth
Jan. 1994, 112 pages, softcover, GAP, avail. 1994, GAP, Color Res, NAPL, RIT T&E

Pocket Pal: A Graphic Arts Production Handbook
Michael Bruno
1992, 234 pages, softcover, Int'l Paper, $6.95, Tools & RIT Bkst

PostScript Language Reference Manual, 2nd edition
Adobe Systems Inc
1990, 764 pages, softcover, Addison-Wesley, $28.95, Addison-Wesley

PostScript Level 2: Communication Handbook
Anonymous
1991, 16 pages, softcover, Adobe, free, Adobe

PostScript Process Color Guide
Agfa Prepress Education Resources
1993, 52 pages, softcover, Agfa, $25, GAP & Color Res

PostScript Screening: Adobe Accurate Screens
Peter Fink
1992, 192 pages, softcover, Hayden, $24.95, GAP & Color Res

Power of Color in Design
Vern Groff
1990, 24 pages, softcover, MIS, $24.95, GAMA

Precise Color Communication
Anonymous
22 pages, softcover, Minolta, free, Minolta

Preparing Your Design for Print
Lynn John
1988, 144 pages, softcover, North Light, $27.95, North Light

Prepress Options Guide
Linnea Dayton
1993, 32 pages, softcover, Agfa, $10.95, Agfa

Prepress Production Video
Anonymous
1990, 14 min., video, GATF, $89, GATF

Prepress Systems—A Guide to Choosing Prepress Equipment
W. A. Dwiggins
1992, 56 pages, hardcover, Linotype-Hell, no charge, Linotype-Hell

Prepress Trade Customs
IPA Committee
1992, notebook, IPA, free, IPA

Principles of Color Design
Wucius Wong
1986, 101 pages, softcover, Van Nostrand, $15.95, Tools

Principles of Color Proofing
Michael Bruno
1986, 396 pages, hardcover, GAMA, $55, GAMA

Principles of Color Reproduction
John A.C. Yule
1967, 420 pages, hardcover, John Wiley, out of print

Principles of Color Technology, 2nd edition
Fred W. Billmeyer, Jr. and Max Saltzman
1981, 240 pages, hardcover, John Wiley, $55.95, John Wiley

Printing Four Color Process on a Duplicator or Small Press
W.S. Mott
1992, 40 pages, softcover, Graphic Ser Pub, $12.50, GAP

Print Production Handbook, The
David Bann
1985, 160 pages, softcover, North Light, $16.95, North Light

Process Color Printing in Newspapers
Irving Pobboravsky, RIT
1987, 76 pages, softcover, Rockwell, free, Rockwell

Quality and Productivity in the Graphic Arts
  Miles Southworth, Donna Southworth and others
  1989, 544 pages, hardcover, GAP, $34.95, GAP, RIT Bkst, RIT T&E, NAPL, & PIA

Quality Newspaper Reproduction
  Anonymous
  1986, 56 pages, softcover, ANPA, $5, ANPA

QuarkXPress 3.0 Handbook, The Official
  Diane Burns and Sharyn Venit
  1990, 506 pages, softcover, Bantam, $26.95, Color Res

QuarkXPress 3.0 Handbook (Windows Edition)
  Diane Burns and Sharyn Venit
  1992, 528 pages, softcover, Bantam, $26.95, GAP

QuarkXPress 3.2 Expert Techniques, Macintosh Edition
  Scott Cook
  1993, 208 pages, softcover, Hayden, $34.95

QuarkXPress 3.2 Expert Techniques, Windows Edition
  Scott Cook
  1993, 208 pages, softcover, Hayden, $34.95

QuarkXPress Book, The, Third Edition/Macintosh Edition
  David Blatner, Keith Stimely and Eric Taub
  1993, 728 pages, softcover, Peachpit, $29, Peachpit

QuarkXPress Book, The, Windows Edition
  David Blatner and Bob Weibel
  1993, 576 pages, softcover, Peachpit, $28, Peachpit

QuarkXPress Handbook, The Official, Macintosh 3.2 Edition
  Diane Burns and Sharyn Venit
  1993, 544 pages, softcover, Bantam, $27.95, GAP & Color Res

QuarkXPress Professional
  Brad Walrod
  1993, 416 pages, softcover, Bantam, $39.95, GAP

*QuarkXPress Tips and Tricks (*Macintosh Edition)
  David Blatner and Eric Taub
  1992, 336 pages, softcover, Peachpit, $21.95, Color Res

QuarkXPress: Visual QuickStart Guide, Mac 3.1 Edition
  Elaine Weinmann
  1992, 200 pages, softcover, Peachpit, $14.95, Peachpit

QuarkXPress: Visual QuickStart Guide, Mac 3.2 Edition
  Elaine Weinmann
  1993, 200 pages, softcover, Peachpit, $15, Peachpit

QuarkXPress: Visual QuickStart Guide, Windows 3.1 Edition
Elaine Weinmann
1992, 200 pages, softcover, Peachpit, $15, Peachpit

Quark XTensions Book, The
Sal Soghoian
1993, 208 pages, softcover, Hayden, $24.95

Quick Printer's Guide to Four Color Process Printing, The
Robert Kiton
1989, 92 pages, softcover, Wild Irishman, $39.95, Wild Irishman

Real World FreeHand 3
Olav Kvern
1991, 512 pages, softcover, Peachpit, $27.95, Color Res

Real World PageMaker 4: Industrial Strength Techniques
Olav Kvern and Stephen Roth
1990, 382 pages, softcover, Bantam, $26.95, GAP & Color Res

Real World PageMaker 5.0: Industrial Strength Techniques (Macintosh Edition)
Olav Kvern, Stephen Roth and Bruce Fraser
1993, 512 pages, softcover, Bantam, $27.95, GAP

Real World Scanning and Halftones
David Blatner and Stephen Roth
1993, 350 pages, softcover, Peachpit, $25, Peachpit

Reproduction of Colour, The
R.W.G. Hunt
1987, 640 pages, hardcover, Fountain Press, $89.95, Tools & RIT Bkst

Resolution
Hans Hartman
1992, disk tutorial, Pixel Ink, $32, Color Res

Scanner Bible, The
Louisa Simone
1993, 420 pages, softcover, disk, Prentice-Hall, $39.95

Scanner Book: How to Make Sellable Color Separations on Any Scanner, The
Randy Zaucha
1991, 100 pages, spiral, Blue Monday, $39.95, GAP

Science and Technology of Appearance Measurement, The
Anonymous
1975, 48 pages, softcover, HunterLab, free, HunterLab

Seeing the Light: Optics in Nature, Photography, Color Vision, and Holography
Falk, Brill and Stork
1985, 464 pages, hardcover, Harper & Row, $54.94, Harper Collins

Seybold Vendor Directory
   Anonymous
   1991, 38 pages, softcover, Seybold, subscription, Seybold

SNAP
   SNAP Committee
   1984, 8 pages, folded, PIA, $6.75, Web Offset Assn

Specifications for European Offset Printing of Periodicals
   FIPP Committee
   1986, 12 pages, softcover, Int'l Fed of Periodical Press, £10, FIPP

Standardised Lithographic Colour Printing: A&B
   Anonymous
   1982, 24 pages, softcover, British Prtg Ind Fed, price not available, Pira

Status of Printing 1989-90
   Michael Bruno
   yearly, 184 pages, softcover, GAMA, $15, GAMA

Story of a Color Picture
   Scitex Educational Videos
   1992, 18 min., video plus 29 page booklet, Scitex, $99.95, GAP & Color Res

Story of a Page, The
   Scitex Educational Videos
   1991, 30 min., video plus 44 page booklet, Scitex, $99.95, SGAUA

Stripping: The Assembly of Film Images
   Harold Peck
   1988, 298 pages, softcover, GATF, $45, GATF

SWOP Manual
   SWOP Committee
   1993, 40 pages, softcover, SWOP, $6.00, Web Offset Assn & IPA

Take a Closer Look
   Kate Hatsy Thompson
   1990, 30+ pages, spiral, Agfa, free, Agfa representative

Test Images for Printing, 3rd edition
   Pamela Groff and Frank Kanonik
   1990, 34 pages, spiral, GATF, $65, GATF

Tone and Color Correction
   Gary G. Field
   1991, 176 pages, softcover, GATF, $60, GATF, GAP, & Color Res

Trap
   Anonymous
   1991, 4 pages, brochure, *Quark Spots and Dots News*, free, Quark

Trapping
  Jim Myrick and Hans Hartman
  1991, disk tutorial, Pixel Ink, $32, Color Res

TRUMATCH Colorfinder
  Steve Abramson
  1990, color chips, fan deck, TRUMATCH, $65, TRUMATCH

Turning the Electronic Page
  1993, 20 min., video, Scitex, $49.95, SGAUA or Scitex

Type and Color
  Alton Cook and Robert Fleury
  1989, 160 pages, softcover, North Light, $39.95, North Light

Using Aldus Freehand 3.0
  Sharyn Venit and Bruce Fraser
  1992, 592 pages, softcover, Bantam, $24.95, GAP

Using Aldus Pagemaker 5.0, 4th Edition
  Douglas Kramer and Roger Parker with Eda Warren
  1993, 544 pages, softcover, Bantam, $27.95, GAP

Using Computer Color Effectively: An Illustrated Reference
  L.G. Thorell and W.J. Smith
  1990, 258 pages, hardcover, Prentice-Hall, $49.95, Prentice-Hall

Using Pagemaker 5 for the Mac
  R. Wallace
  1993, 1100 pages, softcover, Prentice-Hall, $34.95

Using Photo CD for Desktop Prepress
  Frank Cost
  1993, 48 pages, softcover, RIT Res, $12.95, GAP

Using QuarkXPress 3.0
  Tim Meehan
  1990, 340 pages, softcover, M&T, $24.95, Tools

Using QuarkXPress 3.2 for the Mac
  Herr and Qurashi
  1993, 900 pages, softcover, Prentice-Hall, $34.95

Verbum Book of Digital Painting, The
  Michael Gosney, Linnea Dayton and Paul Goethel
  1990, 211 pages, softcover, M&T, $29.95, M&T

Verbum Book of Electronic Page Design, The
  Michael Gosney and Linnea Dayton
  1990, 211 pages, softcover, M&T, $29.95, M&T

Verbum Book of PostScript Illustration, The
  Michael Gosney, Linnea Dayton and Janet Ashford
  1990, 213 pages, softcover, M&T, $29.95, M&T

Visual Nature of Color, The
  Patricia Sloane
  1989, 342 pages, hardcover, Design Press, $29.95, Design Press & Tools

Vital Link—Desktop to CEPS, The
  Anonymous
  1991, 32 min., video, IPA, $295, IPA

Vue/Point: The Hard Copy
  Richard Vinocur
  1991, 1992, 1993 74 pages, softcover, Footprint, $10 each, Footprint

White Paper on Desktop Color: Technical and Marketing Issues
  Kathleen Tinkel
  1990, 170 pages, 3-ring notebook, PrePress Info and Satterthwaite, out of print

X-Rite Tolerancing Poster
  1990, X-Rite, free, X-Rite

Color newsletters

The format for listing the color newsletters is: title, editor, publication frequency, price, publisher and distributor (if different than the publisher).

Aldus Magazine
  Henry Edwards, editor
  bimonthly, 8 issues $24, Aldus Corp.

Cole Papers, The
  David M. Cole, editor
  monthly, $99 yearly, Cole Group

Colorbits
  Lisa Herbert, editor
  four issues per year, free, Pantone

Color Business Report
  Michael Zeis, editor
  monthly, $325 yearly, Blackstone Res

Computer Advantage, The
　　Anonymous editor
　　monthly, $49 yearly + software option, ProMac

Davis Review
　　L. Mills Davis, editor
　　10 times yearly, $300 yearly, Davis

Desktop for Profit
　　Patrick White and Patrick Henry, editors
　　monthly, $95 yearly, NAPL

Desktop Publishing Commentary
　　John Paul Fisher, editor
　　10 times annually, £150 yearly, Pira

Desktop to Press (formerly *The Laser Letter*)
　　Peter Fink, editor
　　occasional, $225 yearly, Fink

Digital Media
　　Denise Caruso, editor
　　monthly, $395, Seybold

Dunn Report, The
　　Thomas Dunn, editor
　　monthly, $195, Dunn Tech

Electronic Cookbook, The
　　Anonymous
　　quarterly, $395, Color Res

Electronic Directions
　　Roger Sperberg, editor
　　3 times per year, free, Electronic Directions

Footprints
　　Richard Vinocur
　　bi-weekly, $175 yearly, Footprint

Future Image Report, The
　　Alex Gerard, editor
　　10 times per year, $245, Future Images

GATF World
　　Thomas Destree, editor
　　bi-monthly, varies, magazine, GATF, members only, GATF

GCA Review, The
　　Vivian Sanchez, editor
　　monthly, free to Graphic Communication Assn. members, GCA

Graphic Communications World
John R. Werner, editor
bi-weekly, $247 yearly, Green Sheet

Images
Henry Hatch, editor
monthly, free to International PrePress Assn. members, IPA

MacPrePress
Kathleen Tinkel, editor
faxed 48 times yearly, $295 yearly, Prepress Info, Subscription service: Color Res

NDCA Journal (National Desktop Color Assn.)
Tyron Lamb, editor
quarterly, free to Typographers Int'l Assn. members, TIA

On Center
Anonymous editor
occasional, free, Schawk

Personal Composition Report, The
Mike Kleper, editor
monthly, $60 yearly, Graphic Dimensions

Quality Control Scanner, The
Miles and Donna Southworth, editors
monthly, $100 yearly, GAP

Seybold Report on Desktop Publishing
Peter Dyson, editor
monthly, $225, Seybold

Seybold Report on Publishing Systems
Stephen Edwards, editor
22 issues yearly, $336, Seybold

Step-by-Step Electronic Design Newsletter
Linnea Dayton, editor
monthly, $48 yearly, Dynamic Graphics

TIA Executive
Typographers Int'l Assn.
monthly, free to Typographers Int'l Assn. members, TIA

%%timeout
Wes Thomas, editor
bi-monthly, free to Assn. of Imaging Ser. Bur. members, AISB

What's New(s) in Graphic Communications
Michael Bruno, editor
bi-monthly, $50, Bruno

Sources of literature

The format for listing the color sources is: name, address and telephone number.

Addison-Wesley: **Addison-Wesley Publishing Co., Inc.**, 6 Jacob Way, Redding, MA 01867; 800/447-2226

Adobe: **Adobe Systems Inc.**, 1585 Charleston Rd., PO Box 7900, Mountain View, CA 94039-7900; 415/961-4400

Agfa: **Agfa Corporation**, 200 Ballardvale St., Wilmington, MA 01887; 508/658-5600

AISB: **Association of Imaging Service Bureaus**, 5601 Roanne Way, Suite 605, Greensboro, NC 27409-2934; 800/844-2472 or 800/962-9480

Aldus Corp.: **Aldus Corporation**, 411 First Avenue South, Seattle, WA 98104-2871; 206/628-2321

Allworth Press: **Allworth Press**, 10 East 23rd Street, New York, New York 10010; 212/777-8395 or 800/283-3572

ANPA: **American Newspaper Publishers Association**, 11600 Sunrise Valley Dr., Reston, VA 22091; 703/648-1212

ANSI: **American National Standards Institute**, 1430 Broadway, New York, NY 10018; 212/642-4935

Automation Eng: **Automation Engineering**, 3617 Indian Queen Lane, Philadelphia, PA 19129; 215/843-5044 or 800/321-5044

Bantam: **Bantam Books**, a division of Bantam Doubleday Dell Publishing Group, Inc., 666 Fifth Ave., New York, NY 10103; 212/765-6500

Barrons: **Barrons Educational Series, Inc.**, 113 Crossways Park Dr., Woodbury, NY 11797

Blackstone Res: **Blackstone Research Associates**, PO Box 314, Uxbridge, MA 01569-0314; 508/278-3449

Blue Monday: **Blue Monday Publishing Co.**, 16601 Lark Ave., Los Gatos, CA 95030; 415/347-5484

Bowker: **R.R. Bowker**, 121 Chanlon Rd., New Providence, NJ 07974; 800/521-8100

Bozek: **Bozek Desktop Inc.**, 327 Severn Rd., Annapolis, MD 21401; 410/849-5232

British Prtg Ind Fed: **British Printing Industries Federation**, 11 Bedford Row, London WC1R 4DX England, UK

Bruno: **Michael Bruno**, 5129 Wedge Ct. E, Bradenton, FL 34203-4029

Business One Irwin: **Business One Irwin**, 1818 Ride Rd., Homewood, IL 60430; 800/634-3966

Chronicle: **Chronicle Books**, 275 Fifth St., San Francisco, CA 94103; 415/777-7240

Coast to Coast: **Coast to Coast Books Inc.**, 1115 SE Stephens St., Portland, OR 97214; 503/232-9772

Cole Group: **The Cole Group**, 2590 Greenwich #9, San Francisco, CA 94123; 415/673-2424

Color Expert: **Color Expert Inc.**, 555 Richmond Street W., Suite 504, Toronto, Ont., Canada M5V 3B1; 416/360-3894

Color Res: **The Color Resource**, 708 Montgomery St., San Francisco, CA 94111; 415/398-5337 or 800/827-3311

Davis: **DAVIS INC**, 2704 Ontario Rd. NW, Washington, DC 20009; 202/667-6400

Design Press: **Design Press**, TAB Books, PO Box 40, Summit, PA; 800/822-8138

Dunn Tech: **Dunn Technology Inc.**, 1855 E Vista Way, Su. 1, Vista, CA 92083; 619/758-9460. *The Dunn Report*: Patrice M. Dunn, 619/758-5401

Durbin: **Durbin Associates**, 3711 Southwood Dr., Easton, PA 18042; 215/252-6331

Dynamic Graphics: **Dynamic Graphics**, 6000 N Forest Park Dr., Peoria, IL 61614-3592; 800/255-8800

EKCo: **Eastman Kodak Co.**, 343 State St., Rochester, NY 14650; 716/724-4000

Electronic Directions: **Electronic Directions, Inc**., 220 E 23rd St., Suite 503, New York, NY 10010; 212/213-6500

FFTA: **Foundation of Flexographic Technical Association, Inc.**, 900 Marconi Ave., Ronkonkoma, NY 11779; 516/737-6026

Fink: **Peter Fink Communications Inc.**, 120 Q St. NE, Washington, DC 20002; 202/832-6886 or 800/551-5921

FIPP: **FIPP** see International Federation of Periodical Press Ltd.

Focoltone: **Focoltone Colour System**, Springwater House, Taffs Well, Cardiff CF4 7QR Wales, UK; 44 0222 810940

Follert: **Melene C. Follert**, 142 E 16th St., 5A, New York, NY 10003; 212/420-1271

Footprint: **Footprint Communications Inc.**, 2337 Lemoine Ave., Fort Lee, NJ 07024; 201/461-5252

Fountain Press: **Fountain Press**, PO Box 11624, Montgomery, AL 36111; 205/281-3854 or **Inspirational Marketing**, PO Box 301, Indianapolis, IN 50125

Future Images: **Future Images, Inc.**, 1020 Parrott Drive, Burlingame, CA 94010; Fax 415/579-0566

GAA: **Gravure Association of America Inc.**, 1200-A Scottsville Road, Rochester, NY 14624; 716/436-2150

GAMA: **Gama Communications**, PO Box 170, Salem, NH 03079; 603/898-2822

GAP: **Graphic Arts Publishing Inc.**, 3100 Bronson Hill Road, Livonia, NY 14487; 716/346-2776 or 800/724-9476

GATF: **Graphic Arts Technical Foundation**, 4615 Forbes Ave., Pittsburgh, PA 15213; 412/621-6941

GCA: **Graphic Communications Assn. (PIA)**, see PIA. *GCA Review*: 703/519-2888

GEF: **Gravure Education Foundation**, 1200-A Scottsville Road, Rochester, NY 14624; 716/436-2150

Graphic Dimensions: **Graphics Dimensions**, 134 Caversham Woods, Pittsford, NY 14534-2834

Graphic Ser Pub: **Graphics Services + Seminars, Inc.**, PO Box 13723, San Luis Obispo, CA 93406; 805/489-9020

Green Sheet: **Green Sheet Communications, Inc.**, PO Box 727, Hartsdale, NY 10530-0727; 914/472-3051

Gretag: **Gretag**, 3917 Orchard Ct., Boulder CO 80303; 303/440-8944 or 800/637-0010

Harper & Row: **Harper & Row**, see Harper Collins

Harper Collins: **Harper Collins Publishers Inc.**, Keystone Industrial Park, Scranton, PA 18512; 717/343-4761 or 800/242-7737

Hastings: **Hastings House Publishers**, 146 Halsteadare, Mamaroneck, NY 10543; 914/835-4005

Hayden: **Hayden**, contact **Prentice Hall Computer**

Henry Holt: **Henry Holt & Co. Inc.**, 115 W 18th St., New York, NY 10011; 212/886-9200 or 800/488-5233

Hoechst Celanese: **Hoechst Celanese**, Print Production Div., PO Box 358, Riverdale, GA 30274; 404/477-2420

Holt, Rinehart & Winston: **Holt, Rinehart & Winston**, 301 Commerce St, Suite 3700, Ft. Worth, TX 76102; 800/782-4479

Horwood: **Ellis Horwood Ltd.,** Market Cross House, Cooper St., Chichester, W. Sussex PO19 1EB England, UK

HunterLab: **Hunter Associates Laboratory Inc.,** 11495 Sunset Hills Rd., Reston, VA 22090; 703/471-6870

Image-In: **Image-In Inc.,** 406 E 79th St., Minneapolis, MN 55420; 612/888-3633

Int'l Fed of Periodical Press: **International Federation of Periodical Press Ltd.,** 35/37 Grosvenor Gardens, Suite 19, London SW1W 0B5 England, UK; 01 828 1366

Int'l Paper: **International Paper**, 6400 Poplar Ave., Memphis, TN 38197; 901/763-6000

IPA: **International PrePress Association**, 552 W 167th St., South Holland IL 60473; 708/596-5110. *Images*: 612/896-1908

John Wiley: **John Wiley & Sons**, 605 Third Ave., New York, NY 10016; 212/850-6000

Linotype-Hell: **Linotype-Hell Corp.**, 425 Oser Ave., Hauppauge, NY 11788; 516/434-3000 or 800/842-9721

Linotype-Hell/Hamilton: see **Linotype-Hell Corp.** for address. **Jim Hamilton**: 516/434-2717

M&T: **M&T Publishing**, contact **Henry Holt**

Macbeth: **Macbeth Corp.**, PO Box 230, Newburgh, NY 12551; 914/565-7660

MacUser: **MacUser Magazine**, 950 Tower Lane, Foster City, CA 94404; 415/378-5600

McGraw Hill: **McGraw-Hill Publishing Co**., 1221 Avenue of the Americas, New York, NY 10020; 212/512-3825 or 800/262-4729

Merritt: **Systems of Merritt, Inc**., 2552 Old Dobbin Drive East, Mobile, AL 36695; 205/660-1240

Micro Pub: **Micro Publishing Press**, 21150 Hawthorne Blvd. #104, Torrance, CA 90503; 310/371-5787

Microtrend: **Microtrend Books**, Slauson Communication, 165 Vallecites de Ore, San Marcos, CA 92069-1436; 800/323-4241

Minolta: **Minolta Corp.**, 101 Williams Dr., Ramsey, NJ 07446; 201/825-4000

MIS: **Management Information Source, Inc.,** PO Box 5277, Portland, OR 97208-5277

Morgan: **Morgan & Morgan, Inc.**, 145 Palisade St., Dobbs Ferry, NY 10522; 914/693-0023

NAPL: **National Association of Printers and Lithographers**, 780 Palisade Ave., Teaneck, NJ 07666; 202/342-0700 or outside NJ 800/642-0225

NCA: **National Composition Assn. (PIA)**, no longer in business, order from GAMA

North Light: **North Light Books**, 1507 Dana Ave., Cincinnati, OH 45207; 800/289-0963

Pantone: **Pantone, Inc.**, ECS Div., 480 Meadow Lane, Carlstadt, NJ 07072; 201/935-5501

Peachpit: **Peachpit Press**, 2414 Sixth St., Berkeley, CA 94710; 415/527-8555 or 800/283-9444

PIA: **Printing Industries of America**, 100 Daingerfield Rd., Alexandria, VA 22314-2888; 703/519-8146

Pira: **The Research Assn. for Paper and Board, Printing and Packaging Industries,** Randalls Rd., Leatherhead, Surrey KT22 7RU England, UK; 44 372 376161

Pixel Ink: **Pixel Ink**, 520 Frederick Street, Suite 13, Berkeley, CA 94710; 415/564-0962

Prentice-Hall: **Prentice-Hall, Inc.,** Englewood Cliffs, NJ 07632; 201/592-2000

Prentice Hall Computer: **Prentice Hall Computer Publishing.**, Simon & Schuster Business and Professional Group, 11711 N. College Ave., Carmel, IN 46032; 317/573-6684 or 800/428-5331

Prentice-Hall Int'l Ltd (UK): **Prentice-Hall Int'l Ltd (UK)**, contact **Prentice-Hall**

Prepress Info: **Prepress Information Service**, 12 Burr Rd., Westport, CT 06880; 203/454-4962

Prepress Tech: **Prepress Technologies**, 2443 Impala Dr., Carlsbad, CA 92008; 619/931-2695

Prtg Mgmt Serv **Printing Management Services**, PO Box 46, San Luis Obispo, CA 93406: 805/543-5968. Orders: BookMasters Distributions Services; 800/247-6553

ProMac: **ProMac**, PO Box 13267, Oakland, CA 94661-3267; 800/822-2289

Quark: **Quark Inc.**, 300 S Jackson, Suite 100, Denver, CO 80209; 303/934-2211

Random House: **Random House Inc.**, 201 E. 50th Street, 31st Fl., New York, NY 10022; 212/751-2600 or 800/726-0600

Rich: **Rich & Associates**, PO Box 678, Olney, MD 20830-0678; 301/774-1771

RIT Bkst: **Rochester Institute of Technology**, Campus Connections (Bookstore), PO Box 9887, Rochester, NY 14623; 716/475-2501

RIT Res: **Rochester Institute of Technology Research Corp.**, 75 Highpower Road, Rochester, NY 14623; 716/475-2883

RIT T&E: **Rochester Institute of Technology**, Technical & Education Center, Order Dept., PO Box 9887, Rochester, NY 14623; 716/475-2739

R.K. Prtg Pub: **R.K. Printing and Publishing Co.**, 120 Fifth Ave., Montgomery, WV 25136

Rockport: **Rockport Publishers**, 146 Granite St., Rockport, MA 01966; 508/546-9590

Rockwell: **Rockwell International Corp.**, Graphic Sys. Div., 3100 Central Ave. South, Chicago, IL 60650; 708/850-5600

Satterthwaite: **Satterthwaite and Associates**, see Prepress Info

Schawk: **Schawk, Inc**, 1695 River Road, Desplains, IL 60018; 708/827-9494

Schiffer: **Schiffer Publishing Ltd.**, 1469 Morstein Rd., West Chester, PA 19380; 215/696-1001

Scitex: **Scitex America Corp.** 8 Oak Park Dr., Bedford, MA 01730; 617/275-5150

Scott Foresman: **Scott, Foresman and Company**, 1900 E Lake Ave., Glenview, IL 60025; 708/729-3000

S.D. Warren: **S.D. Warren Paper Co.**, 225 Franklin St., Boston, MA 02110

Seybold: **Seybold Publications**, PO Box 644, Media, PA 19063; 215/565-2480

SGAUA: **Scitex Graphic Arts Users Assn.**, PO Box 290249, Nashville, TN 37217; 800/858-0489

SPIE: **The International Society for Optical Engineering**, PO Box 10, Bellingham, WA 98277-0010; 206/676-3290

SWOP: **Recommended Specifications for Web Offset Publications**, see PIA; 703/519-8146, or IPA

Sybex: **Sybex**, 2026 Challenger Dr., Alameda, CA 94501; 800/227-2396

TAGA: **Technical Association of Graphic Arts**, PO Box 9887, Rochester, NY 14623; 716/272-0557

Tektronix: **Tektronix Inc.**, PO Box 1000, MS 63-630, Wilsonville, OR 97070; 800/835-6100

TIA: **Typographers International Association**, 2233 Wisconsin Ave. NW, Suite 235, Washington, DC 20007; 202/965-3400

Tools: **Tools of the Trade**, 3718 Seminary Rd., Alexandria, VA 22304; 703/823-1919

TRUMATCH: **TRUMATCH Inc.**, 331 Madison Ave., New York, NY 10017; 212/351-2360

USA Today: **USA Today**, 1000 Wilson Boulevard, Arlington, VA 22209; 703/276-3400

Van Nostrand: **Van Nostrand Reinhold Company**, 115 Fifth Ave., New York, NY 10003; 212/254-3232

Watson-Guptill: **Watson-Guptill Publications Co.**, 1 Astor Plaza, 1515 Broadway, NY 10036; 800/451-1741

Web Offset Assn: **Web Offset Assn (PIA)**, see PIA; 703/519-8146

Wild Irishman: **The Wild Irishman, Inc.**, 4634 Warrensville Center Rd., Cleveland, OH 44128

Winchcombe: **Winchcombe**, 43A Richmond Rd., London SW20 0PG England, UK; 081 946 6993

Xerox: **Xerox Corporation**, 100 Clinton Ave. S. Rochester, NY 14604; 716/423-5090

X-Rite: **X-Rite, Inc.**, 3100 44th St. SW, Grandville, MI 49418; 616/534-7663

Yale: **Yale University Press**, 92A Yale Station, New Haven, CT 06520; 203/432-0940

Ziff-Davis: **Ziff-Davis Publishing Company**, 764 Gilman Street, Berkeley, CA 94710

INDEX